The Evolution of Project Management in a Scaled Agile Environment

Kerry R. Wills

Copyright © 2018 by Kerry R. Wills

All rights reserved. This book or any portion thereof may not be reproduced or used in any manner whatsoever without the express written permission of the publisher except for the use of brief quotations in a book review or scholarly journal.

First Printing: 2018

ISBN 978-1-387-92122-5

Kerry R. Wills
Southington, CT 06489

http://kerrywills.wordpress.com

Preface 4
Acknowledgements 7
About the Author 8
1. What is Agile? 11
    1.1 Agile Development 13
    1.2 Scaled Agile 16
2. Evolution of Delivery 21
    2.1 Evolved Delivery Landscape 21
    2.2 Project Management Implications 27
    2.3 Evolved Portfolio Landscape 32
    2.4 Hypotheses 37
3. Evolution of Projects 39
    3.1 Scope Decomposition 39
    3.2 Aggregation of Information 41
    3.3 Information Sharing 43
    3.4 Evolved Definition of a Project 45
4. Evolution of the Project Manager 48
    4.1 Scaled Agile Roles 58
    4.2 Competencies 63
    4.3 The Evolved Project Manager 69
5. Evolution of the PMO 76
    5.1 Why We Need a Lightweight PMO 79
    5.2 What is a Lightweight PMO? 82
    5.3 Putting Our PMOs on a Diet 95
6. Aligning Agile and Portfolio Management Principles 103
    6.1 Scaled Agile Principles 103
    6.2 Portfolio Management Principles 116
    6.3 Aligning the Principles 126
7. Key Concepts 130
    7.1 The Delivery Model has Changed 130
    7.2 It is Not an "or" Conversation 131
    7.3 Agile is Not an Excuse 137
    7.4 Anchor on the Principles and Align Coaching 139
    7.5 It Has Always Been About the People 142
    7.6 Revisit the Hypotheses and Conclusions 145
References 150

Preface

There is significant movement in the technology delivery landscape that has been happening for the last few decades, and it is shaking up organizations across many industries. Agile started as a delivery methodology for development teams to release code quicker; specifically in the web development space where stakeholders wanted to see visual representations earlier and to be able to iterate many times. Agile then evolved into a larger construct which encompassed entire organizations. This is known as "scaled agile" or "enterprise agile" which includes organizational constructs and roles, governance models and portfolio functions.

There are several popular scaled agile methodologies but they all have similar approaches and constructs. For purposes of this book, I will leverage the most popular model called the Scaled Agile Framework also known as SAFe ® (Leffingwell 2017). Written approval was received to reference the SAFe model and readers should use the website (www.scaledagileframework.com) as the primary source of information on the framework. Note that SAFe and Scaled Agile Framework are registered trademarks of Scaled Agile, Inc.

When people first look at this model they will notice that there are no roles which have the title "project manager" nor does it look like there are "projects" in the framework. This may lead some to believe that this means that project management concepts, principles and skills are not needed. Note that I will not go deep into the scaled agile model, as there is significant material in the marketplace which covers that so I do expect that the reader has a basic understanding of the framework and concepts.

I am both certified in project management (PMP) as well as scaled agile (Scaled Agile Framework Agilist) and plan to demonstrate how the project management principles and skills are critical but need to evolve with the model. It is not choosing agile or project management; they are both needed for successful delivery. I will lay out four key hypotheses and then demonstrate them throughout the book.

The intention of this book is to propose a dialogue between the project management world and the scaled agile world and to demonstrate that it does not have to be either model; they can both exist and be complimentary to each other. Project management principles, competencies and techniques are needed in the agile world and agile principles and practices can be applied to evolve the effectiveness of the project management world. I would encourage the reader to become familiar with the scaled agile principles and model to form their own hypotheses on the alignment with project management.

Acknowledgements

It is important to recognize those people who helped and supported me to write this book which is my sixth on project management concepts.

- My wife, Diane, for supporting me in my many endeavors
- My children, Stephanie and Matthew, who inspire me every day to be the best that I can be
- My parents for instilling in me the values to think creatively, trust my instincts and to follow my dreams
- My colleague, Nick Pettinelli, for reviewing the content and providing valuable counsel
- The many team members that I have worked with who provided me many of the insights that are collected in this book

About the Author

Kerry Wills has worked as a Consultant and a Program Manager for Fortune 500 companies on multi-million dollar technology programs since 1995. During that time, he has gained experience in several technology delivery capacities; as a portfolio manager, program manager, project manager, architect, developer, business analyst, and tester. Having worked in each of these areas gives Kerry a deep understanding of all facets of an Information Technology program. Kerry has planned and executed over $2 Billion of IT programs as well as assessed and remediated several troubled programs. Recently, Kerry helped to lead the transition to Scaled Agile for a Fortune 100 company.

Kerry is a member of Mensa and has a unique perspective on project work, resulting in eleven patents, published work in project management journals and books, and speaking engagements at dozens of project management conferences and corporations around the world.

As a thought leader in the project management domain, Kerry has written five prior books focusing on various aspects of project management. These all build on each other, anchor on a consultative approach and are the foundation for many of the concepts proposed in this book.

1. Focusing on the evolving skills required for project managers to be successful in the current delivery landscape (Essential Project Management Skills in 2010)
2. Running programs using a "consultative approach" consisting of eight core principles (Applying Guiding Principles of Effective Program Delivery in 2013)
3. Conducting project and program assessments for troubled projects or to perform reviews (Assessing IT Projects to Ensure Successful Outcomes in 2015)
4. Establishing programs with a structure that can endure the long duration of delivery (Establishing an Enduring IT Program in 2016)

5. Highlighting the need for project management skills to evolve and proposing a new competency model with 30 significant competencies (The Consultative PM: An Evolved Model for Project Management Competencies in 2017)

1. What is Agile?

The term "agile" is used in many ways by many people when discussing technology delivery. It is important to recognize that people mean different things when they use this term. I think about the definition of "agile" in three primary categories:

1. Agile as a delivery methodology for development teams

Agile development has been around for decades and focuses on the specific ceremonies and approach that a development team takes to deliver work in an agile manner. This is where we have constructs such as iterative development, product backlogs, scrum teams and stand up meetings. This methodology focuses specifically on a team and, in many cases, they work within a larger project or program which is traditionally managed.

2. Agile at scale for organizations

While the first bucket focuses at the team level, scaled agile is much broader and focuses on all levels of a delivery organization and an enterprise. It encompasses teams which span other delivery teams and also includes portfolio-level functions and shared services which support many teams. Therefore this is a much more holistic model which requires a robust transformation of an entire company to operate in.

3. Agile principles

There is a core set of agile principles which apply across the delivery universe that can be applied to many different teams and models. These include things like collaboration, a focus on teams, failing fast and design thinking. These will be reviewed in detail later in the book.

Many people confuse the three categories or even combine them into one big category. It is important to recognize the difference between these categories and be clear in communications as to what focus is being discussed. For example, any team can leverage agile principles (#3) even if they are not operating like a scrum team (#1). Also, some organizations may choose to have teams deliver using agile ceremonies (#1) but not go beyond the team level in a scaled agile organizational model (#2).

While the content in this book assumes that the reader has some basic understanding of agile, it is important to ground on some of the key concepts so that the hypotheses about project management can be made within the proper context. For that reason, this chapter will present an overview of the key aspects of scaled agile models.

1.1 Agile Development

In the 1990s, the approach to develop technology was evolving and gave rise to constructs such as scrum and extreme programming (XP). There was recognition that the classic "waterfall" approach to development was long and prone to costly mistakes found later in the lifecycle. In 2001, a group of software developers met in Utah and drafted what is known as the "agile manifesto" as a guide for agile software development which is outlined below (Agile Alliance, 2010).

We are uncovering better ways of developing software by doing it and helping others do it. Through this work we have come to value:

- *Individuals and interactions **over** processes and tools*
- *Working software **over** comprehensive documentation*
- *Customer collaboration **over** contract negotiation*
- *Responding to change **over** following a plan*

That is, while there is value in the items on the right, we value the items on the left more.

These values contributed to the agile development approach which has several key characteristics.

- A scrum team is comprised of cross-functional resources who work across many functions
- Iterative development which assumes rework and revisiting of functionality based on reviews
- These iterations are organized into short time-boxed periods, known as "sprints" or "iterations" (generally taking 2-3 weeks in duration)

- At the end of the iterations are a review with stakeholders, known as a "demo"
- Daily meetings known as "stand up" meetings to discuss progress and any risks (blockers)
- Work is organized into User Stories and Tasks which align to specific functional increments of time and is expected to drive value to the overall product
- Quality is embedded in the process and leverages specific tools and techniques such as continuous integration and automated testing
- The concept of "servant leadership" where the leader's role is to coach and support the team

Many companies have adopted the agile development approach and organized into scrum teams which follow the principles and ceremonies outlined above.

1.2 Scaled Agile

Over the last decade, several models have arisen which take the agile principles and apply them to constructs beyond the delivery team level. These are known as "enterprise agile", "agile at scale" or simply "scaled agile." These models recognize that just having agile delivery teams work in traditional organizational models is not optimizing the value and approach thus needing the entire enterprise to evolve in order to more appropriately support the teams and goals of the organization.

While there are several scaled agile models, they all have similar constructs with a multilayer view. Figure 1.1 shows a simplified view of the levels and based on the Scaled Agile Framework (Scaled Agile Framework version 4.5 2018).

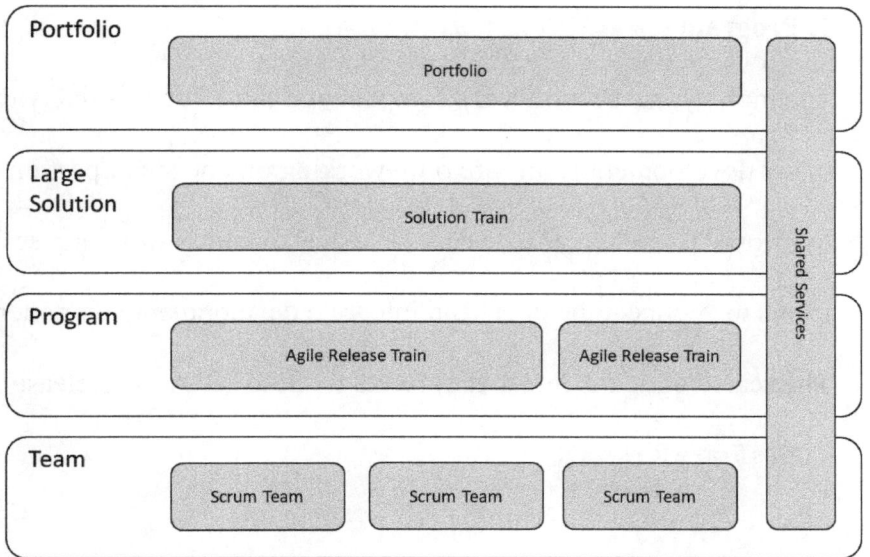

Figure 1.1 Scaled agile levels

There are generally four levels to the scaled agile model (starting from the bottom of the framework and working upwards) plus a set of shared services which span all of the levels:

1. Team

This is the classic agile development team (scrum) which operates with the core agile principles and ceremonies. This is the primary focus of the model and where the delivery of work is performed and drives overall value.

2. Program

Technology has become very complex and therefore it is likely that many development teams are only working on one small portion of the work. Therefore, there needs to be teams which work across other teams to "connect the dots" and integrate development components. The scaled agile model (SAFe) refers to these as "Agile Release Trains" or ARTs.

3. Large Solution

Because of increasing technology and product complexity, many technical solutions span multiple organizations and teams/ARTs and so it is important to have a layer over the entire end-to-end solution. Note that this level only exists under certain scenarios when a solution is very complex and spans multiple organizations and therefore requires some additional coordination and planning.

4. Portfolio

Generally, companies will organize their technology investments into pools of funding and resources, which are considered portfolios. This function aligns to organizational constructs and is accountable to the Enterprise for the investments and delivery of work aligned to the company strategies. This includes the intake, prioritization and decomposition of the strategies into scope as it flows through the delivery framework. Also within this level is a set of coordination and reporting activities that are performed within the Lean Portfolio Management function.

Shared Services

There is a group of services which work across each of the levels, generally perform work within the delivery teams and also perform "core" work that they do as an organization. While these functions may be specific to the organization, examples of these teams could include information security or architecture.

Each of these levels has specific roles, ceremonies, processes and deliverables. The intention is for prioritization and sequencing to flow down the model and for information to aggregate back up the model. The intention is also to have the work and most of the resources at the team level delivering on the work and more "lightweight" functions as you move up the model.

2. Evolution of Delivery

As agile has become more pervasive and agile at scale is increasing in popularity, the landscape of technology delivery has changed significantly. This has had impacts on how work is structured, the concept of a project and traditional project management techniques and responsibilities.

2.1 Evolved Delivery Landscape

The scaled agile models has several fundamental changes to how work gets organized, managed and delivered. It is important to recognize these changes so that we can highlight how the project management functions and principles need to change to align with them. Some of the significant model changes are outlined in this section.

It is all about the team

The team is at the center of the universe in the agile world. When reading the scaled agile frameworks, they are presented bottom up starting with the team and then working their way up the levels. This is because the team is where the work is performed and where the value is created.

In these team-based models the intention is to maximize value and delivery and to minimize overhead and governance. This is the opposite approach from the traditional top-down models where there are heavy centralized governing and controlling functions and the project manager tells people what to do. The models do recognize that there is some need for governance and therefore refers to these as "lightweight" portfolio management functions.

Having a team-based model with lightweight portfolio management means that organizations need to assess the amount of overhead, reporting, governance and management functions that exist and look to optimize their models to reduce a lot of this and leverage tools and automation for reporting. Remember the manifesto: *individuals and interactions **over** process and tools.*

There is a flow of work and information

Scaled agile models have a logical flow of work with a decomposition of scope down the levels. Each level of the model has a work intake function which takes in work and then prioritizes and sequences it based on value.

At a high level, scope gets identified within a portfolio work intake function. There are several techniques for prioritizing and sequencing the work, but they generally focus on delivering the most value as early as possible. This work then gets decomposed as it moves down the model into the subsequent levels where it gets broken into smaller groupings of scope, prioritized, sequenced and worked on.

Each level has an intake function and a backlog of work which gets continually prioritized and sequenced. At the lowest level, each of the teams is simply working their backlogs like cooks in a kitchen taking orders. To continue with this analogy, they do not know who ordered the food or even what the full meal looks like; they just keep cooking.

As scope decomposes down the model and gets worked on, information flows back up the model. Starting at the bottom of the framework, the teams highlight progress and blockers for their work which gets raised to the next level to be aggregated, as appropriate. This allows for the highest level of stakeholder reporting to occur on progress towards strategic goals and milestones.

The intention is to use a work management system so that this information is automated and not a burdensome process (i.e. lightweight management). The intention is to highlight these items as part of "doing the work" in the tracking system and then discuss at the respective ceremony.

Funding of persistent teams

Traditional funding was focused on projects with a (mostly) defined scope and schedule. In the scaled agile model, funding is focused on longstanding (persistent) teams and it is the scope that is variable based on the prioritization and sequencing of work. If additional capacity is needed for the team to take on more work, then additional funding gets allocated to that team based on the appropriate portfolio review.

The concept of persistent teams is important to the scaled agile model. Part of the value of the agile model is improved velocity (productivity) of the team which is a result of them working together over a long period of time.

Working on a cadence

Agile delivery is organized into iterations (also known as sprints), which are generally two weeks long. Those iterations are then grouped into higher increments which generally include five iterations (roughly ten weeks of time). The intention is for work to be broken down into small "chunks" which get released in these iterations and increments.

Within these periods of time are several agile ceremonies which could include demonstrations, reviews of prior work for improvements (retrospectives), planning time and even time to innovate. The intention is for all teams to work on the same cadence and to repeat the sequence over time and continue to improve, which is where the velocity improvements are realized.

Information is not pushed

In scaled agile models, there is not a formal status report document which gets sent to hundreds of people. Instead, the progress of work is captured within a delivery management tool as part of the ceremonies and work cadence. If people want to understand the progress against scope elements, the work tool can be used to highlight this in a real-time manner. There are also demonstrations of working capabilities but those are meant for reviews to tie-in the value being delivered, and not for providing a status readout.

Decentralized decision making

The scaled agile approach relies on decision making at the team level and not an escalation of authority to a central group or person, except for strategic decisions. The intention is to keep decisions with the team members who are closest to the knowledge and context and therefore are best informed. Also, keeping decisions at a local level not only makes for better outcomes but also a faster process since there is not the need for formality and multiple stakeholder reviews beforehand.

2.2 Project Management Implications

The changes to the delivery approach highlighted in the last section have significant implications to project management concepts. Table 2.1 highlights some of the changes from the traditional project model to a scaled agile model.

Table 2.1 Summary of changes

Area	Traditional	Scaled Agile
Scope Management	Fixed scope for a project which gets defined up front and baselined	Constant prioritization and sequencing of scope aligned to value

Area	Traditional	Scaled Agile
Change Management	Any changes to scope or schedule go through a governance process with impacts and approvals	Constant prioritization and sequencing
Governance	Phase gates and approvals to proceed	Frequent demonstrations and iterations with acceptance criteria
Financial Management	Tied to approved projects and specific defined scope with variance reporting	Tied to persistent teams and capacity
Schedule Management	Maintain a roadmap of milestones and activities with dependencies	Milestones aligned to scope elements and aggregations of iterations
Resource Management	Specialized and move between projects as work starts and stops	Dedicated to persistent teams and do many functions

Area	Traditional	Scaled Agile
Business Involvement	Heavy in the beginning then drop off during development then pick up for testing	Constant involvement throughout the lifecycle in ceremonies and demos

Each of these changes has implications to project management concepts which need to be recognized and considered when working in the new framework.

Scope

Work is now prioritized and sequenced in a multiple levels of backlogs and longstanding teams work down the list. This means that work is no longer defined up front and organized into a finite set of scope documents aligned to a project and funding. It also means that scope can change (or be reprioritized) often based on organizational priorities and the identification of value.

Changes

Since the focus of work is on prioritization and sequencing aligned to value, there is no longer a need to focus on controlling and managing changes. The approach is dynamic and occurs as part of the agile ceremonies and therefore a centralized inventory of changes is no longer needed.

Governance

Since agile is about empowering teams and iterative development, the days of formal phase gates are gone. The focus changes to demonstrations of working capabilities and iterations of development with specific acceptance criteria.

Financial Management

Funding moves from being tied to scope to being tied to capacity of persistent teams. This will present challenges when attempting to track the costs of specific scope items or initiatives. This change will also have implications on the approach for corporate accounting including depreciation, write-offs of assets and capitalization of software.

Schedule Management

The new model aligns milestones to scope elements such as User Stories and Features. With frequent reprioritization of scope it becomes hard to maintain a milestone roadmap especially for multi-year strategies which span many teams. Dependencies are still a critical component of agile delivery, but it becomes more difficult to manage when the work is federated out to different autonomous yet interdependent teams.

Resource Management

The resource management approach fundamentally changes with scaled agile. The model moves from people being mobile between teams as the work and projects progress to a focus on dedicated resources on persistent teams. This should make the tracking of resources and capacity planning easier for an organization while reducing the amount of resource manager roles.

2.3 Evolved Portfolio Landscape

While the delivery landscape has certainly evolved with scaled agile which has changed how project management operates, we must also recognize that the portfolio landscape has evolved. Scaled agile models still recognize the need for a "portfolio" of work but the structure and functions have changed.

Here are a few ways that the portfolio functions change in the new delivery framework.

- Scaled agile proposes a "lightweight" approach to portfolio management based on the focus on teams and value. This means that large centralized PMOs are no longer appropriate and a leaner approach is required to facilitate transparency and delivery progress.
- The Portfolio becomes a "hub" in a hub-and-spoke model with the delivery teams and scope elements as the "spokes." The hub is very light but still supports working across the hubs.

- Portfolios are no longer about central control of work so much as aggregations of scope, funding and reporting in a decentralized model that focuses on the teams. They will need to help "connect the dots" across the various teams and levels.
- Portfolios still have the same portfolio management functions but they operate differently. For example, instead of managing financials based on scope it now needs to be aligned to persistent teams. These changes will be covered later in the PMO chapter of this book.
- Reporting will need to change with the evolution of PMO functions which includes the use of authoritative tools to coordinate and track delivery
- This evolution needs to be part of a larger companywide effort and will have interim phases which need to be recognized and planned for

With the evolution of the scaled agile delivery frameworks, the portfolio level performs three primary functions, which are outlined in Figure 2.1.

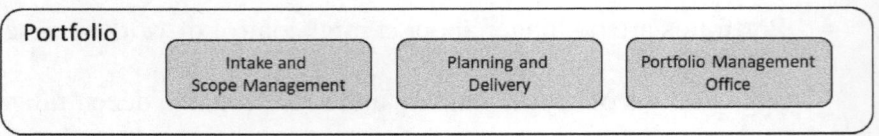

Figure 2.1 Portfolio level functions

1. Intake and Scope Management

The primary focus of the Portfolio level is to facilitate the prioritization and movement of scope through the delivery levels.

- Work Intake – Receive and inventory work requests in the delivery pipeline. The portfolio should shepherd the process to assess work based on a set of criteria, approve or deny work, determine the delivery structure and update key sources of information.

- Pipeline and Backlog – Maintain a prioritized backlog of all requests and current work which includes Themes and Portfolio Epics. Facilitate the ongoing prioritization of work.

- Scope Documentation and Traceability – Manage a comprehensive Portfolio Backlog of scope which traces to multiple levels in the delivery framework.

2. Planning and Delivery

While pure agile suggests that teams are simply working a backlog of scope, I do believe that large companies will still require roadmaps for new products, complex solutions and corporate strategies. These multiyear roadmaps will need to be coordinated across the delivery portfolio and over time.

- Multiyear Planning – Maintain the multiyear views of benefit realization and key delivery or value driving milestones for roadmaps.
- Lightweight Program Management – Plan and track discrete elements of scope throughout the delivery levels and operating model. This includes tracking, reporting risk/issue management, and communications. This may also include the facilitation of removing any impediments to delivery across teams.
- Lightweight Governance – Govern the investments through portfolio stakeholder meetings, as appropriate. This may mean facilitating prioritization and tradeoffs across different stakeholder owners.

3. Portfolio Management Office

While the delivery of scope and value will take place at the lower levels of the model, the portfolio management office will still need to aggregate key portfolio information and communicate it to senior stakeholders.

- Portfolio Tracking and Reporting – Aggregations and transparency of portfolio metrics including financial reporting, resource reporting, vendor reporting, milestone reporting, issue/risk reporting, decisions and status. They may also facilitate reviews and follow ups as appropriate.

- Stakeholder Communications – Portfolio-level stakeholder communications including progress and risks aligned against milestones and value realization.

- Enterprise Alignment – Even in scaled agile organizations, there are still enterprise functions which will require some coordination with the delivery portfolio. The PMO can support these activities which could include requests from compliance areas, audit functions or accounting needs.

2.4 Hypotheses

This delivery model evolution is in the early stages of maturity and many companies are just starting their transitions. However, given some of the themes and beliefs within the delivery community, I would submit four hypotheses regarding scaled agile and project management which will be explored throughout the remainder of this book.

1. *There are still projects, but their definition changes*
2. *There is still the need for project management competencies*
3. *There is still the need for portfolio management office functions, but they evolve*
4. *The agile principles can be applied to project and portfolio management*

Each of these hypotheses will be expanded upon in the subsequent chapters and examples will be used to demonstrate their validity. Some of these statements may be controversial but this approach is meant to create a dialogue between the traditional project management world and the agile world. Therefore, the zealots on either side will likely find tactical nuances and inconsistencies in the examples but I would ask to focus on the intention which is to demonstrate how both models are needed for success in the evolved delivery environment.

3. Evolution of Projects

Scaled agile models propose that work is continuously flowing and being prioritized at multiple levels which therefore suggests that there is no longer the traditional concept of a project. This chapter will unpack that premise and look at how work is organized, decomposed and federated down the levels of the model and then aggregated back up.

3.1 Scope Decomposition

In the scaled agile model, scope starts at the top and then flows down the levels, being decomposed into further detail and smaller units of work. The following figure visually depicts this breakdown of scope along the main levels of the framework along with the associated scope element which are based on the SAFe model (Scaled Agile Framework version 4.5 2018). It also shows each of the intake functions, as noted with funnel icons.

```
Portfolio      [Theme Backlog]    [Themes]
               [Epic Backlog]     [Portfolio Epics]

Large
Solution       [Epic Backlog]     [Program Epics]

Program        [Epic Backlog]     [Program Epics]
               [Feature Backlog]  [Features]

Team           [Story Backlog]    [User Stories]
```

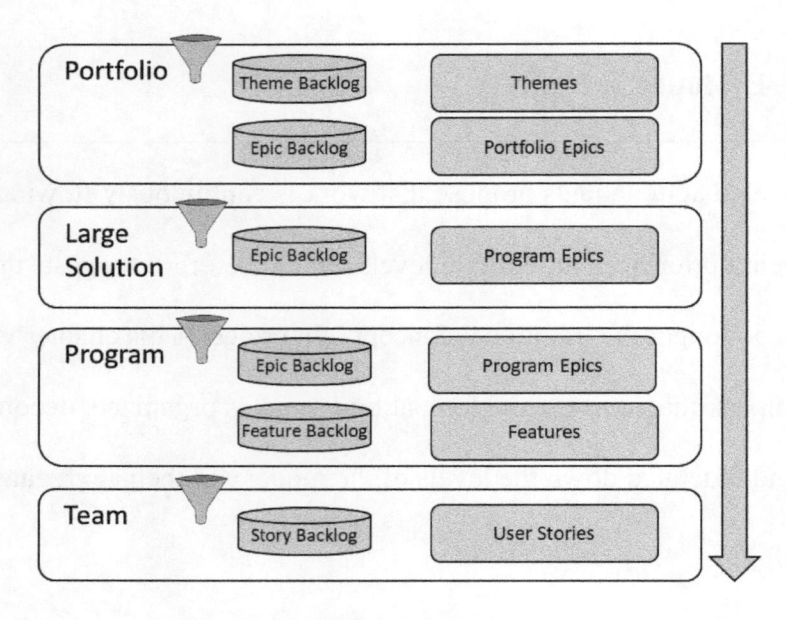

Figure 3.1 Scope decomposition

At the highest level (Portfolio), a Strategic Theme is identified which aligns to an enterprise strategy. Themes are then broken down into Portfolio Epics which have specific solutions that span multiple iterations, contain a business case and get tracked in the portfolio backlog.

Portfolio Epics then get decomposed further into Program Epics which are managed within the program or solution backlogs for the Agile Release Trains or Solution Trains to manage. Note that this image highlights that Program Epics can be worked on at the Large Solution Level or the Program level in the scaled agile model depending on whether there is a Large Solution or not.

This scope and work then get further refined into Features and User Stories at the Team level. This is the smallest unit of work and gets managed within the team backlog.

3.2 Aggregation of Information

At the lowest level in the framework, scope is contained in User Stories which should align to a specific scrum team and take one iteration (generally 2-3 weeks in duration) to complete. Teams update the respective work management tool to track progress for User Stories and then participate in ceremonies such as stand up meetings to discuss risks and issues, known as blockers.

Figure 3.2 shows this alignment at the Team level for User Stories, iterations, funding and progress tracking. It also shows that similar methods are used in the higher levels of the framework as work is aggregated.

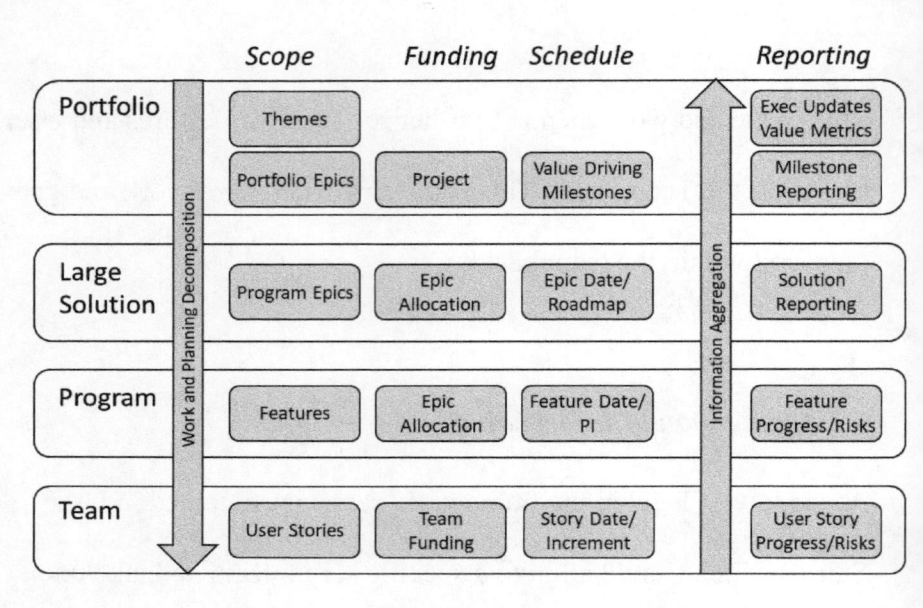

	Scope	Funding	Schedule	Reporting
Portfolio	Themes			Exec Updates Value Metrics
	Portfolio Epics	Project	Value Driving Milestones	Milestone Reporting
Large Solution	Program Epics	Epic Allocation	Epic Date/ Roadmap	Solution Reporting
Program	Features	Epic Allocation	Feature Date/ PI	Feature Progress/Risks
Team	User Stories	Team Funding	Story Date/ Increment	User Story Progress/Risks

(Work and Planning Decomposition ↓ / Information Aggregation ↑)

Figure 3.2 Aggregation of information

At the Program level, Agile Release Trains are comprised of several delivery teams and focus on Features which get developed within a specific Program Increment (which is generally comprised of five iterations and is therefore roughly ten weeks long). Agile Release Trains also track progress and risks across the interconnected delivery teams.

Large Solutions manage Program Epics which span across several delivery teams and the timeframes within the delivery cadence. They are able to compile the relevant information to report against the overall solution roadmap.

Because of this upward information flow combined with the traceability of the elements at each level, the Portfolio function is able to provide insight into strategic roadmaps, value realization and key milestones.

3.3 Information Sharing

Section 3.1 demonstrated how work starts with a Theme and decomposes down to the team level with a User Story. Section 3.2 then showed how work and the progress are then aggregated back up the model. As the scope decomposes down and work gets aggregated back up, there is a need for reporting against the different dimensions of the work. Note that this is not classic reporting where a status documents gets sent to several hundred people each week.

Within the scaled agile framework there are several needs for sharing of information to various stakeholders.

- Since User Stories roll up into Features which inform Agile Release Trains, there is a need to report on progress of these User Stories and Iterations
- Since Features roll up into Program Epics for Release Trains or Solution Trains, there is a need to report on progress of these Features and Program Increments
- Since Program Epics roll up into Portfolio Epics, there is a need to report on progress of Program Epics
- There are portfolio-level stakeholders that are interested in the health of the portfolio and will have several reporting needs such as value realization against the investment and progress towards strategic goals
- Companies will still have strategic roadmaps and will therefore want to understand progress towards those roadmaps

3.4 Evolved Definition of a Project

This chapter has highlighted how scope flows through the levels of the scaled agile model and then how information is aggregated back up because of the associations between the planning and scope elements. Within the framework, the most significant portfolio-level scope element is the Portfolio Epic which has several key characteristics:

- It aligns to a specific company strategy and milestone(the Strategic Theme)
- It is aligned to a specific stakeholder owner who has accountability for the delivery of the work and value (the Epic Owner)
- It is focused on an initiative which spans multiple teams and increments
- There is a lean business case associated to the scope of a Portfolio Epic
- It is the key scope element which gets prioritized and sequenced within the Portfolio backlog

When looking at this list, we could observe that the characteristics identified above are similar to the characteristics of a project. And, like a project, portfolio-level stakeholders will be looking for an understanding of progress against strategic initiatives and roadmaps that are informed by Portfolio Epics.

In the traditional project delivery environment, a project was the center of the universe with a set of specific scope, milestones and funding which was approved and reported on with a regular cadence. In the scaled agile environment, there is still the concept of an initiative with many of the characteristics of a project, however, the operating model is very different and it is the teams that are the center of the universe.

In this new world, the definition of a project becomes an aggregation of scope and funding aligned to realizing the expected value of a specific strategic initiative. Because the scope traces from the bottom to the top of the model, financial aggregation can occur by knowing which teams are working on which User Stories and then rolling their cost (resource capacity) up to the appropriate Portfolio Epic. Milestones also become an alignment related to the sequencing of the associated User Stories, Features and Epics with their respective planned timeframes of delivery.

4. Evolution of the Project Manager

On the surface, when looking at scaled agile models there do not appear to be any roles with titles similar to that of a project manager. This may lead some practitioners to believe that project management roles are not part of the framework or needed in the new delivery model.

Beyond looking at the framework, there is the position with many purist agile practitioners that project managers primarily work across siloed organizations and when you remove those silos in a scaled agile environment, you no longer need project managers. Even worse, there is a suggestion that they could still support administrative activities which is nowhere near the value that these resource can bring to an organization. This chapter will explore the reasons why project management type people are still needed and then highlight how the scaled agile roles require project management competencies to be successful.

First, let's start with three statements regarding the current delivery environment, which I believe strongly in based on nearly 25 years in technology delivery. I will introduce these statements and then describe them as a means to demonstrate the need for roles to support them.

1. Solutions continue to dramatically increase in complexity and require roles to connect the dots
2. Self-organizing teams cannot perform magic
3. We have to recognize and accommodate for human nature regarding work

1. Solutions continue to dramatically increase in complexity and require roles to connect the dots

The business landscape is increasing in complexity every year as companies become more competitive, customers seek more personalized products and technology solutions become more innovative. This increasing complexity has several material impacts on the delivery of company strategies.

In my last book on evolved project management competencies, I presented an outline of the areas which were increasing in complexity and their impacts on delivery (Wills 2017). Figure 4.1 highlights some of the areas which are increasing in complexity.

- Business Products – With customers becoming more demanding, the marketplace is moving more towards individualized solutions and companies are offering more specialized products. The result is having many versions of products or solutions that have features that can be customized.
- Technology Solutions – Technology continues to evolve and innovate with new solutions, vendors, programming languages and packaged software released frequently. These solutions then become interrelated with other technologies and solutions.
- Organizations – As business products become more complex and companies continue to grow, so does their organizational structure. Multiple divisions are set up to manage the different aspects of the business (e.g. Sales, Finance, Product, Reporting, and Compliance). Each division has its own goals, management and approach for conducting business.

- <u>Process and Tools</u> – To accompany evolving business products, technologies and organizations is the need for evolved processes and tools to govern, manage and report on delivery.

Complexity
- Business Products
- Technology Solutions
- Organizations
- Process and Tools

⇒

Delivery Impacts
- More Complex Solutions
- More Delivery Partners and Stakeholders
- Matrixed Delivery Models
- Specialized Roles

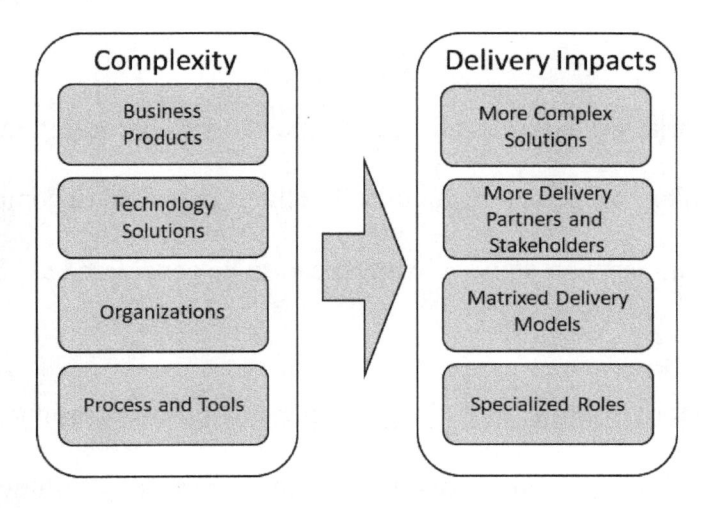

Figure 4.1 Increasing complexity with associated impacts

Also for my last book, I conducted a survey of 337 project management professionals to solicit input on these hypotheses of increasing delivery complexity. When asked if they thought that the complexity of the delivery environment has changed over the last five years, the responses were overwhelmingly "yes" (Wills 2017).

- 75% of respondents said that products are getting more complex
- 89% said yes to technology becoming more complex
- 70% said yes for organizations becoming more complex
- 68% said yes for processes and tools becoming more complex

Now that we have established that the work is becoming more complex, we need to recognize that these increases in complexity have impacts on delivery which need to be considered as outlined in Figure 4.1.

- <u>More Complex Solutions</u> – Increasing business product and technology complexity are creating complicated solutions with many organizational handoffs and integration points. This requires more focus on integration planning, developing solutions with more interfaces and testing across the many connections.
- <u>More Delivery Partners</u> – As organizations grow larger and their solutions become more complex, there are more partners involved in delivery who need to be coordinated with. This could be internal organizations, strategic delivery partners, software vendors or consultants.

- <u>Matrixed Delivery Models</u> – Because of evolving organizational structures, delivery structures are becoming more matrixed with resources reporting to multiple leads. This will evolve in the scaled agile model as resources become more dedicated to persistent teams, but there will likely still be shared resources who matrix into delivery teams.
- <u>Specialized Roles</u> – Evolving product and technology solutions require resources to become specialized in specific business areas, technology components or delivery roles. It is becoming more challenging for any one person or role to understand an entire solution end-to-end.

As demonstrated above, the increasing complexity has significant impacts on delivery which requires someone to 'connect the dots' across the teams, stakeholders, and delivery partners who are generally federated out across many different delivery teams and organizations.

2. Self-organizing teams cannot perform magic

Agile has a core principle around "self-organizing teams" which is primarily focused on the teams and empowering them to make decisions and take on work as opposed to waiting for direction. This concept makes a lot of sense within the team. However, if you believe the first statement around complexity combined with the agile practice of having teams with a smaller number of people then there must be a realization that most solutions will require an abundance of interdependent teams.

With this environment of many interdependent teams, there would seem to be an underlying set of assumptions that the work "magically" comes together:

- Teams *magically* know their interdependencies and proactively coordinate with their partner teams
- Solutions *magically* come together across multiple teams, interfaces and technologies
- Milestones and interdependencies *magically* get coordinated to provide an end-to-end view

- Changes in prioritization and sequencing of work *magically* cascade to interdependent teams

For the record, I do not believe in magic. Note that I am being somewhat cynical and am not suggesting that these activities are not holistically performed by the teams but I am suggesting that empowered teams are naturally focused on optimizing their internal focus and do not always stay on top of the moving parts that are connected to other teams. There is a need for a coordinating function to ensure that interdependencies, milestones and solutions get managed end-to-end across the many teams otherwise they will likely not be performed optimally or at all.

I have a real example of this scenario. A few years ago I had taken over a large program which had an annual budget of over $100M. The teams were set up as Agile Release Trains and all had their associated work, milestones and scrum teams. In the first meeting that I attended, Team A had reported that they were on track to meet their milestones and they were in a green status. After they presented, six other interdependent teams reported that they were at significant risk because of dependencies on Team A to complete work earlier than their current plan. In this model, Team A was not incented to care about their downstream dependencies and focused on their specific goals, which included reporting on their green status. The other teams had no influence over Team A's schedule or priorities and were dependent on them. No one was managing these interdependencies and the teams clearly were not communicating as much as they should have been.

Beyond not coordinating with their schedules, from a solution perspective, when the teams did deliver their work there were significant quality problems because the solutions were not congruent across the domains. Data was inconsistent and there was fallout which took more than one year to remediate.

Within the first few months, I had restructured the initiative to identify roles which were accountable across the teams to ensure planning and solutions were considered holistically.

3. We have to recognize and accommodate for human nature regarding work

Developer skillsets are focused heavily on technology delivery and not necessarily soft skills. This is why many of them do not want to go into management, communicate with other resources and may even have challenges working with non-technical resources.

Also, there are many team members who just want to be told what to do. Some of this may be engrained within a corporate culture but I do believe that some of it is the nature of certain people. They are great at what they do and just want someone to point them in a direction. So if we move to a model of empowerment and self-organizing teams and do not recognize the nature of these resources, we may be setting up the team for failure. The resources may not have the interest or skills to operate in a fully autonomous model without some support and direction.

I believe all of the aforementioned statements to be true about the environment that we work in, the nature of teams and the nature of people which all leads to the conclusion that there is a fundamental need for roles to coordinate work end-to-end. However, I am not suggesting that we need traditional project managers who manage in a top-down or "command and control" approach, but I am suggesting that we still need people with the competencies to complement the agile roles and make them more successful, many of which (I would strongly argue) are those same competencies that make a successful project manager as well.

4.1 Scaled Agile Roles

At each level of the Scaled Agile Framework, there are significant roles that should be viewed as requiring project management type skills and competencies. Five of them are listed in Table 4.1 (Scaled Agile Framework version 4.5 2018). The intention of this section is not to recreate the framework, so much as identify the key responsibilities as a baseline from which to highlight the relevant competencies and then to compare them to consultative project management competencies.

Table 4.1 Key scaled agile roles

Level	Role
Team	Scrum Master
Team	Product Owner
Program	Release Train Engineer
Large Solution	Solution Train Engineer
Portfolio	Lean Portfolio Management

Scrum Master

At the Team level, the Scrum Master is the primary facilitator of delivery. Their responsibilities span many areas of working with the team:

- Facilitate work through the delivery process aligned to the stated goals and priorities
- Facilitate the team-level agile ceremonies including stand up meetings, backlog refinement, retrospectives and iteration planning
- Act as the primary focal point for team communications

- Coordinate the removal of any identified barriers to progress which could include escalating to higher levels in the models, if appropriate
- Organize the work in the delivery management system and ensure that the information is maintained
- Coordinate planning and dependencies with other teams, as needed

Product Owner

The Product Owner works with scope on a scrum team. Their primary responsibility is to define and prioritize User Stories within the team backlog. Their other responsibilities include the following:

- Organize the team backlog to ensure that User Stories are identified, documented with relevant information, prioritized and sequenced properly for delivery
- Support iteration planning to represent the objectives and acceptance criteria of the User Stories
- Participate in the demonstrations of iteration capabilities to key stakeholders

Release Train Engineer

These resources are accountable for coordinating the delivery of value within a specific Release Train at the Program level. Their responsibilities include many functions since Release Trains have several stakeholder interactions that span business domains and technology domains.

- Coordinate planning and delivery dependencies across the associated teams
- Facilitate Program Increment planning with key business stakeholders (e.g. Product Management) and technical stakeholders (e.g. System Engineers)
- Coordinate Release Train risk and issue resolution which includes escalations, as appropriate
- Facilitate the appropriate ceremonies for planning, demonstrations and reviews
- Coordinate communication to relevant Program-level stakeholders

Solution Train Engineer

The Solution Train Engineer is accountable for facilitating the delivery of work across a solution which spans multiple teams and Release Trains. Similar to a Release Train Engineer, these resources have to coordinate between business and technical domains and stakeholders.

- Coordinate planning and delivery dependencies across the associated teams and Release Trains
- Facilitate planning with key business stakeholders (e.g. Solution Management) and technical stakeholders (e.g. Solution Engineers and Architects)
- Coordinate cross-solution risk and issue resolution which includes escalations, as appropriate
- Facilitate the appropriate ceremonies for planning, demonstrations and reviews
- Coordinate communication to key stakeholders

Lean Portfolio Management

In the scaled agile model, portfolio management is a function and not a specific role. This function has several responsibilities which align to coordinating activities and providing transparency across the scaled agile portfolio.

- Align delivery and scope (Themes) to the appropriate corporate strategies
- Facilitate the portfolio-level scope intake and prioritization through the portfolio backlog
- Coordinate funding for the dedicated teams aligned to solutions
- Coordinate the portfolio office functions including reporting on milestones, funding and delivery
- Coordinate key portfolio metrics

4.2 Competencies

Based on the set of responsibilities listed in the prior section, a collection of themes start to emerge regarding the competencies required for each role.

Scrum Master

The scrum master role is primarily a facilitation role that works with the team to deliver on the prioritized work which drives value. Therefore, this role requires proficiency in planning and consultative competencies, such as:

- Iteration planning and coordination
- Alignment of work within iteration schedule and identification of dependencies
- Facilitation of scope prioritizing and sequencing (backlog)
- Coordination of resources and vendors for delivery
- Risk and issue coordination including removing any impediments
- Diligence and attention to detail regarding delivery tracking
- Communications
- Negotiation of priorities and scope
- Facilitation of progress, agile ceremonies and decisions
- Leading, coaching and motivating team members to optimize performance and morale
- Fundamental understanding of the business scope and technology solution

Product Owner

The Product Owner role focuses on the scope of the team which also requires some consultative competencies.

- Scope prioritizing and sequencing within the delivery timeframes
- Decision making regarding scope
- Ownership of scope and value realization
- Communications of scope and priorities
- Influencing and negotiating stakeholders on key scope decisions
- Facilitation of scope decisions and prioritization which could span different stakeholder groups
- Strong business acumen

Release Train Engineer

The Release Train Engineer has to have many strong competencies because they drive delivery, but also have to coordinate with business and technical stakeholders.

- Program Increment planning and executing with multiple stakeholders
- Coordination of teams for delivery

- Alignment of schedule and dependencies across teams and iterations
- Scope prioritizing and sequencing across multiple teams (backlog management)
- Risk and issue coordination including removing impediments to progress
- Diligence and attention to detail regarding tracking of delivery elements
- Communications to multiple stakeholders
- Negotiation of priorities and scope
- Facilitation and ownership of work, ceremonies and decisions across multiple teams and iterations
- Leading and motivating multiple stakeholders and team members to optimize performance and morale
- Solid understanding of both the business scope and technology solution

Solution Train Engineer

The Solution Train Engineer is accountable for the delivery of large solutions which span many teams and Agile Release Trains and therefore is the role which requires the strongest set of planning and consultative skills.

- Solution planning and executing across multiple stakeholders, teams and timeframes
- Alignment of schedule and dependencies across iterations and teams
- Scope prioritizing and sequencing across multiple teams (backlog management)
- Coordination of multiple teams for delivery
- Risk and issue coordination including removing impediments to progress
- Diligence and attention to detail regarding solution delivery tracking
- Communications to multiple stakeholder groups
- Negotiation of priorities and scope across multiple teams and stakeholders

- Facilitation and ownership of work, ceremonies and decisions across multiple teams and iterations
- Leading and motivating multiple stakeholders and team members to optimize performance and morale
- Advanced understanding of the business scope and technology end-to-end solution

Lean Portfolio Management

The roles within the lean portfolio management function focus primarily on portfolio-type activities but do require some consultative competencies since their work spans multiple stakeholder groups and teams.

- Facilitation of portfolio planning and alignment of scope to strategy
- Prioritization and sequencing of scope across multiple teams (portfolio backlog management)
- Coordination of milestones and dependencies to align to portfolio commitments and value realization
- Coordination of funding within the portfolio

- Facilitation of the resolution for any escalated risks or issues
- Diligence and attention to detail regarding portfolio metrics and reporting
- Communication to portfolio stakeholders
- Facilitation and negotiation of portfolio-level decisions and priorities

4.3 The Evolved Project Manager

In my prior book I introduced the concept of a "Consultative Project Manager" which identified a set of core competencies that are proposed to be critical for project managers in today's delivery environment. There were thirty competencies identified which were then grouped into four categories, identified in Table 4.2 (Wills 2017).

Table 4.2 Categories of competencies

Category	Description
Project Management Fundamentals	Working understanding of project management deliverables, processes and tools in domain areas such as financial management, schedule management, resource management and scope management
Consultative Skills	Using "soft skills" and self-awareness to influence, facilitate, communicate, motivate and collaborate with project stakeholders
Business Acumen	Having an understanding of the business and industry that the project is delivering for
Technical Acumen	Having an understanding of the technology solution and assets that the project is delivering

Associated to each of these four categories is a set of competencies which are proposed to be needed for project managers to be successful with a key focus on the "consultative" skills area. I believe that these competencies are also the same ones needed for the scaled agile roles to be successful. Figure 4.2 shows the mapping of agile roles to these competencies. When presented visually, it becomes clear that the key scaled agile roles require competencies in each of the planning, consultative and acumen categories (R is required and N is nice to have). It also becomes evident that because their roles span different stakeholders and teams, both the Release Train Engineers and Solution Train Engineers roles require strong consultative skills.

Competency	Scrum Master	Product Owner	RTE	STE	Portfolio
PM Fundamentals					
•Planning and Executing	R		R	R	R
•Scope and Change Management	R	R	R	R	R
•Schedule Management	R		R	R	R
•Resource Management	R		N	N	N
•Vendor Management	R		N	N	N
•Financial Management	N		N	N	R
•Risk and Issue Management	R		R	R	R
•Decision Management	R	R	R	R	R
•Delivery Methods	R	N	R	R	R
•Professionalism and Ethics	R	R	R	R	R
Consultative					
•Self-Awareness	R	N	R	R	
•Ownership	R	R	R	R	N
•Diligence	R		R	R	R
•Attention to Detail	R	R	R	R	R
•Build Relationships and Influence Stakeholders	R	R	R	R	R
•Communications	R	R	R	R	R
•Learning Agility	R		R	R	
•Judgment and Critical Thinking	R		R	R	
•Leadership and Motivating	R	R	R	R	N
•Conflict Management and Negotiation	R	R	R	R	R
•Facilitation	R	R	R	R	R
•Innovation	N		N	N	
•Customer Focus	R	R	R	R	R
Business Acumen	R	R	R	R	N
Technical Acumen	R		R	R	N

Figure 4.2 Scaled agile role competency alignment

If we anchor on this core set of competencies for comparison, it becomes evident that the competencies required for successful project managers are the same ones required for successful scaled agile roles. This means that resources who are consultative project managers today and who possess these skills can successfully transition into roles in the scaled agile model.

It is important to note that this comparison of competencies does not mean that there is a one-to-one correlation between the two types of roles. That means that we cannot say that all project managers working on a team should immediately become scrum masters and all program managers should become Release Train Engineers. An assessment should be performed of the competencies of each individual and the resulting skills should be aligned to the needs of the role. Some examples of this mapping include the following scenarios:

- Resources with strong project management fundamental skills could consider supporting some of the lightweight portfolio functions

- A resource with strong business orientation could become a Product Owner
- Someone with a strong technical background, fundamental project management and facilitation skills may become a good Scrum Master
- Resources with strong consultative skills, program management fundamentals and relevant business or technical acumen could move into a Release Train Engineer or Solution Train Engineer role

Beyond having the relevant competencies we need to understand that there also needs to be a change in mindset with some our resources. Some of them likely had success in a traditional model that was managed top down and where they controlled all aspects of their project and the work. They now need to align to the "servant leader" concept where their role is to support the team and not to drive or control.

Lastly, we need to recognize that not every existing project management resource would be a good match for these new agile roles. People who may be considered traditional project managers that have historically managed using a "command and control" style are unlikely to be successful in the new team-oriented model that requires softer influencing and motivating techniques. However, I would argue that these people are probably not that successful in today's matrixed project delivery environment either since it also requires those softer skills. In any case, whether in the changing environment of "standard" project delivery or the scaled agile world, project managers need to evolve their skillsets.

This chapter has demonstrated that the scaled agile model requires roles to connect the dots across the many delivery teams and levels and that the scaled agile roles require people who demonstrate proficiency in the competencies of planning, consultative skills and acumen. These competencies are the same ones displayed by the most successful project managers in the matrixed world of project delivery today. Therefore, as companies transition into the scaled agile models, they can leverage many of their project management resources to fulfill the key roles (assuming that they already possess those identified competencies).

5. Evolution of the PMO

Over time, the size and complexity of programs have increased and driven the need for central governance over the work of those programs. Historically, these programs would have a large Program Management Office (PMO) with dedicated resources to manage each of the core functions (finance management, resource management, schedule management, communications management, risk and issue management, vendor and contract management, scope management, etc.). This information would be shared with the many stakeholders involved in a program.

Also, as complexity increased, delivery became organized into portfolios of multiple interrelated programs and was coordinate by a Portfolio Management Office (also called PMO). As we evolve into a scaled agile delivery model with the concept of lightweight portfolio management, it seems that a robust PMO is no longer considered necessary for success, or at least no longer sustainable in a leaner environment.

There are two premises proposed and explored in this chapter regarding PMO functions:

1. There is still the need for PMO functions in a scaled agile model, but these functions must evolve
2. These functions can be managed in a lightweight PMO

There is still the need for PMO functions in a scaled agile model, but these functions must evolve

I do not believe that in a corporate environment that we will ever get to the aspirational model where delivery is simply a set of autonomous self-organizing teams working down a continuously reprioritized backlog of work. In a corporate environment there will always be the need for business metrics such as return on investment as well as the need to have transparency into progress towards strategic initiatives and milestones. PMO functions provide this insight; however, I do believe that these functions will need to evolve their approaches in the scaled agile model.

Chapter 5.1 will go into further detail into the need for PMO functions in a corporate environment and why a PMO is still needed. Chapter 5.2 will then highlight how these functions will need to evolve in the scaled agile model. Note that for purposes of this chapter, I will use the term "PMO" to represent both a Program Management Office and a Portfolio Management office since they coordinate the same functions.

These functions can be managed in a lightweight PMO

As of writing this book, I am currently running a portfolio which is funded for several hundred millions of U.S. Dollars of delivery and I am running it with a two person portfolio office. We still manage the same functions listed previously but do it in a much more efficient, automated and value-focused manner. Also when I speak to some of my counterparts who are running large initiatives and portfolios they also seem to be moving in the same direction with smaller portfolio management teams.

Chapter 5.3 will propose some techniques for putting PMOs "on a diet" to become more lightweight but still provide the needed transparency and support to the overall portfolio.

5.1 Why We Need a Lightweight PMO

There are several themes in the scaled agile framework that align to the current corporate environment and the need for driving key portfolio functions.

- <u>Return on Investment</u> – Increasingly, companies are investing significant amounts of funding into technology and strategic delivery and senior leaders will need to understand how the value from these investments is being realized. This requires tracking how the investments are being made and capturing the value being realized.
- <u>Strategic Initiatives</u> – Because of increased competition and shareholder expectations, companies are pursuing aggressive strategies. There is a need for transparency of how these initiatives are progressing towards their goals. This requires information on

progress against milestones and budget as well as communication of risks and issues.

- Competing Priorities – Companies do not just have one strategy nor do they have one set of stakeholders with one agenda. There are still many competing priorities and agendas which require some governance to facilitate the selection of optimal strategies to drive value.

So, while many of the portfolio functions are still needed today, there is also a set of trends pushing these functions into a "lightweight" portfolio model:

- Focus on Value – In a scaled agile model, the primary focus is on delivering business value and not on functions or roles that may be perceived as overhead and not directly contributing to the realization of benefits.
- Maturity of Delivery – As delivery models mature and the quality of delivery improves, the need for centralized control, reporting and governance decreases as the accountability transitions to the teams.

- <u>Evolving to Scaled Agile</u> – One of the fundamental concepts of scaled agile is called "lean portfolio management" which has several key components; all of which decrease the need for a large traditional Program Management Office:
    o Decentralized governance – The primary focus is on the delivery teams being empowered, being self-managed and having accountability instead of a centralized governing and controlling model.
    o More frequent releases – The intention is to no longer have annual planning cycles or large one-time releases, so there is not as much need to coordinate large activities in a centralized manner.
    o Funding teams – Funding moves from scope-based in a traditional delivery model to capacity-driven teams, which means that there is less need to centrally manage scope, changes and resources.

5.2 What is a Lightweight PMO?

Based on the trends identified in the prior section, the Portfolio Management Office needs to evolve from a centralized controlling organization into more of a lightweight team that facilitates transparency and coordination across the levels and teams within the delivery portfolio. Even in a scaled agile model there is still the need to report on progress, risks, milestones, and value so I do not think that the function goes away entirely. In fact, I believe that the scaled agile model requires more diligence and transparency to manage the many moving parts, which is where the tools and automation play a pivotal role.

Portfolio Management Office Functions		
Strategy and Investment Planning	Scope and Change Management	Financial Management
Schedule Management	Risk and Issue Management	Decision Management
Resource Management	Vendor Management	Communication and Reporting
Business Case Management	Controls and Audit	Operations

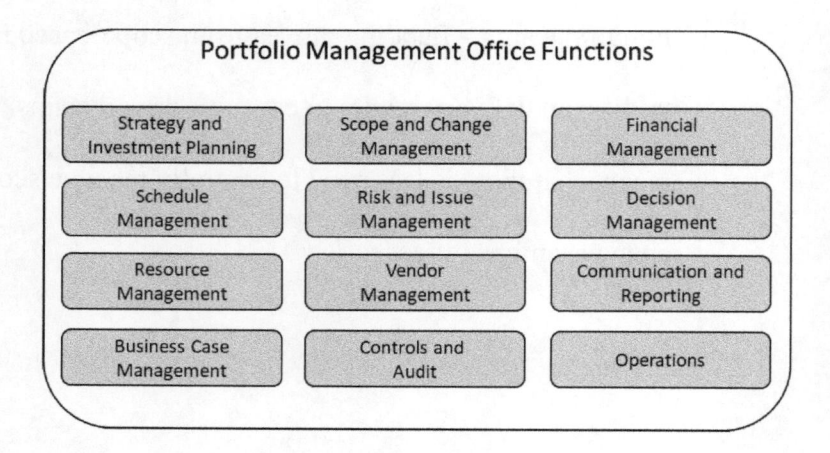

Figure 5.1 PMO functions

Figure 5.1 highlights the primary 12 functions that a PMO supports. Although a Portfolio Management Office still needs to exist, the functions that it performs will need to evolve because the delivery operating model is rapidly changing. This evolution of accountabilities is highlighted in the following sections.

Strategy and Investment Planning

In a traditional PMO, this function centralizes the strategic and investment planning through an annual planning cycle, which generally starts in the second quarter of the year and then takes the remainder of the year to complete. The planning approach includes identifying all possible work and ideas, collecting estimates and the expected value for the work, presenting it to a governance committee and then determining which areas get funded based on a set of criteria. Once approved, more detailed planning and reviews are performed to assess resource needs and create the milestones and dependencies to deliver the work.

The scaled agile model focuses on connecting the work to the enterprise strategy and then funding persistent teams to work down an inventory of work based on a set of strategic priorities and continuous planning. While there is still a need to facilitate this process, it is not a centralized coordination function and so the approach is much more streamlined and efficient. It is also not an annual process so much as a continual process of prioritization and sequencing.

Scope and Change Management

In a traditional PMO, scope and changes are managed centrally and rigorously. This includes the intake and approval of scope that is aligned to programs and projects and requires forums with many stakeholders to negotiate and agree upon the definition. Once that scope is defined and baselined, a robust change management process is used to review and approve any proposed changes along with their associated impacts.

In scaled agile, scope and priority is determined at the Portfolio level and aligned to strategic objectives. As scope decomposes down, each level of the framework has an intake function, backlog refinement and prioritization process. There is clear accountability for the scope in the solution management and product management functions. There is also no need for change management since there is no longer the concept of "baselined" scope and funding aligns to teams and not to work.

Financial Management

Financial management involves a rigorous set of tracking methods in the traditional Portfolio Management Office. This includes maintaining a budget for each program and project, tracking progress against those budgets and then robust reporting on variances, capitalization and other accounting needs. This generally requires many meetings and reviews with the various finance and accounting organizations and resources.

There are also financial assessments and estimates for new scope and proposed changes. This financial planning process aligns to the annual planning and funding cycle and therefore many of these processes are repeated each year.

In the scaled agile model, funding is allocated based on strategic planning and primarily aligned to persistent teams and shared services. Reporting will aggregate information from each level using the work management tools and therefore robust processes and teams are not needed. Variability in financial reporting also decreases significantly since it is a capacity-based model and not a scope-based model.

Schedule Management

Schedule management is also a rigorous process in a traditional PMO. This involves breaking down the work into milestones, activities and tasks. Schedule management also includes identifying and managing the critical path of key milestones which drive value, as well as aggregating milestones across projects and programs including the tracking of cross-program dependencies. Lastly, the schedule impacts of any proposed change are assessed and updated as changes are approved.

In the scaled agile model, milestones are aligned to specific scope elements such as Themes and Portfolio Epics and are coordinated through the time-boxed schedule of iterations and increments. These milestones and dependencies are managed and tracked within the delivery software as part of the agile planning and operating ceremonies.

Risk and Issue Management

In a traditional model, risks and issues are coordinated and tracked at the project, program and portfolio levels. There is centralized management for the identification of items, assessing impacts and monitoring the required actions to remediate them. There is also centralized reporting of the risks and issues through status reports and stakeholder meetings.

In the scaled agile model, risks and issues are facilitated at each level of the framework during the specific planning and reviewing ceremonies. The framework also provides an escalation path up the levels in the model as needed. Risks and issues are captured in the context of the how work is performed within scope elements and ceremonies and so there is no need for any additional management or governance.

Decision Management

In a traditional PMO, key decisions are tracked and managed centrally across the portfolio. Many times, the PMO will have to facilitate the decision making process across multiple teams and stakeholders to negotiate a resolution which can be difficult given competing agendas and priorities.

In scaled agile, the decision authority is part of the delivery framework at each level but a key tenant is that decisions are made as low in the model as possible. There are specific roles which are accountable for prioritization of work and decision making in regards to that work. For example, the Product Owner role has decision making authority for the scope and prioritization of the work for a particular team. The empowerment of resources to be able to make decisions also plays heavily into a more evolved decision making process.

Resource Management

A traditional PMO centrally coordinates program and project resources and sometimes facilitates the planning and acquisition of key resources. This function includes managing a roster of team resources and governing the process to identify and staff those resource needs based on scope and changes to that scope. Also in a traditional model, resources are aligned to separate organizations that oftentimes have resource manager roles who negotiate with the portfolios to coordinate the needs and timing of the resources within their organization.

In the scaled agile model, resource planning is performed based on team capacity and business priority. Since funding is directed towards persistent teams, resources are dedicated at the team level and there is significantly less mobility of resources between teams. Resources are also expected to perform multiple roles. For all of these reasons, there is less of a need for a governing process and for resource management roles.

Vendor Management

Many delivery portfolios and teams leverage external vendors or partners to augment roles or to deliver specific components of a solution. Aligned with the financial management process, Portfolio Management Offices have historically manage vendor contracts and invoices. At times, the PMO may even coordinate vendor selection and planning.

Scaled agile recognizes vendors as a critical component to delivery. While PMOs will still likely need to track vendor contracts and costs/invoicing, the selection and management of vendors is coordinated at the team level.

Communications and Reporting

A traditional PMO has a centralized model for cross-portfolio communication and reports on the status of progress and risks against scope, schedule and cost. They also aggregate status for multiple enterprise and stakeholder reporting needs. Because large companies have multiple governing functions, it is likely to have several different report templates, formats and meetings even if the information is similar and this requires PMO resources to coordinate the different needs and documents.

In the agile world, progress is obtained through the maintenance of delivery information in tracking software as work gets performed and as part of conducting the respective ceremonies. Large Solutions may generate reports against specific scope or commitments. The enterprise functions will have to evolve or learn new ways to obtain information as the lightweight approach does not support multiple status reporting models and formats.

The traditional PMO facilitates weekly portfolio status meeting, weekly leadership meeting and other stakeholder meetings with relevant attendees. Because they are centrally coordinated and span complex programs, some of these meetings can contain a significant number of people even if only a few people are actually presenting content. Preparation for status meetings also generally requires pre-meetings and team-level status meetings and so the process compounds itself.

In the scaled agile model, multiple person status meetings are replaced by agile ceremonies (e.g. stand up meetings, refinements and system demonstrations). These smaller forums are more like working sessions and are focused on delivery and working functionality. They only contain people who are contributing to the delivery of the work and associated value. They also leverage existing tools and information that is used to manage the work and so less preparation is needed.

Business Case Management

The traditional PMO maintains the program or portfolio business case of value realization and cost and tracks performance against that business case. This includes tracking the cost of delivery as well as the realization of the expected benefits to ensure that the return on investment gets realized.

In scaled agile, Portfolio Epics can have a lightweight business case that includes expected investment, success criteria and expected benefits. These are maintained by the Epic Owners.

Controls and Audit

In the traditional PMO model and corporate compliance environment, delivery risks are reviewed with internal and external audit teams to determine exposure and then plans are created to close these risks. The PMO generally coordinates the audit reviews with the subsequent implementation and communication of associated controls throughout the delivery portfolio.

In the scaled agile model, controls should be coordinated at each level of the delivery model. Note that the audit and compliance functions will have to evolve their approach accordingly as well since many of their controls require phase-gate approvals which are no longer part of the delivery model. They should look for things such as acceptance criteria and demonstrations to confirm acceptance from key stakeholders.

Portfolio Operations

Beyond the functions identified above, the Portfolio Management Office also supports many operational activities across the delivery portfolio. This can include activities such as the onboarding of resources, assignment of seats, coordination of meetings and conference rooms, planning offsite sessions and maintaining document repositories. Many of these activities are still required to be performed in a scaled agile model and need to be supported in some capacity.

Summary

Figure 5.2 summarizes the PMO functions to demonstrate that they are still needed but they will evolve and require much less effort to manage (noted by the color).

PMO Function	Traditional Model	Scaled Agile
Strategy and Investment Planning	Centralized planning with annual planning cycles and rigorous prioritization process	Align work to strategies and prioritize at different stakeholder levels
Scope and Change Management	Central management with robust process for changes	Continuous prioritization and sequencing of work
Financial Management	Maintaining budgets and tracking variances	Funding teams and capacity
Schedule Management	Tracking milestones, dependencies and impacts	Milestones aligned to scope and work cadence
Risk/Issue Management	Coordinated and tracked at multiple levels	Coordinated and tracked at multiple level
Decision Management	Track and facilitate key decisions	Decision authority at each level
Resource Management	Coordinates program resources	Done at team level aligned to capacity
Vendor Management	Manage vendor contracts and invoices	Track cost of vendors
Communications and Reporting	Robust communication and reporting	Aggregation of information from work tools and ceremonies
Business Case Management	Maintain business case	Lightweight business case aligned to Epics
Controls and Audit	Coordinate risks reviews and closure	Controls at each level, but likely some work
Operations	Coordinate portfolio operations	Portfolio operation support

Effort: High | Medium | Low

Figure 5.2 Summary view of differences in the PMO functions

5.3 Putting Our PMOs on a Diet

Chapter 5.2 demonstrated how the PMO functions are evolving within a lightweight Portfolio Management Office as companies move towards the scaled agile model. Therefore, a plan needs to be established to put our traditional program offices "on a diet" to make them more lightweight. The following four step process outlines an approach to do this.

1. Assess the PMO functions

The first step is to gather information that will assist in analyzing the portfolio management office functions. There is no single answer for what a lightweight PMO should look like and therefore every team and organization needs to understand some important information before planning their diet. Some of this information includes the following:

- Inventory the functions currently performed by the PMO to have an understanding of what services and capabilities are being offered
- Inventory the current stakeholders that are customers of PMO functions; who are they and what information do they receive from the PMO

- Document how the organization plans to evolve into a scaled agile manner and where the PMO functions will be managed within the model
- Inventory the evolving needs of the organization, delivery teams and key stakeholders including key information, reporting or services

2. Analyze the information

Once the relevant information is gathered, analysis should be performed to align the planned delivery model and stakeholder needs with the activities that need to be performed within each of the respective PMO functions. The end result should be a mapping of PMO-type functions and activities to the organizations and delivery teams.

After this mapping is conducted, the team should assess the needs of the stakeholders to determine what is really critical to delivering value. The intention should not be to simply move the functions to a different part of the organization but to really consider value, effort and accountability with the desire to have a minimum set of capabilities that satisfy the highest value needs. Therefore it is likely that many Portfolio Management Office functions or services will be discontinued or reduced with respect to the amount of responsibilities that they manage.

Note that many PMO activities and deliverables are developed as a response to broader corporate governance and requests such as developing various status reports to comply with enterprise demands. In these cases, the analysis should also evaluate these enterprise needs to determine if they are critical and if there are more efficient ways of meeting them.

3. Plan and implement the evolved approach

Based on the analysis of needs, a plan should be created for each of the PMO functions. This plan will likely have several possible types of actions which are listed below:

- <u>Stopping work</u> – Some functions may not make sense in a scaled agile model and should be stopped. For example, the need for centralized status reports may go away as teams work in authoritative tools and update progress as part of how they work. In these cases the plan should document how to stop the work, what happens to the team members and close any "loose ends" that need to be completed.

- Transitioning accountabilities – Many traditional PMO functions are performed by delivery teams in a scaled agile model. For example, managing milestone dependencies may be better aligned to teams which span across delivery teams (e.g. Release Trains) and not centrally coordinated. For these functions, the plan should document how the functions will operate in the model, what the new accountabilities are and how/when and to who the function gets transitioned.

- Evolving the approach – In some cases, the PMO will retain the function but it will need to evolve. For example, financial management evolves from tracking cost aligned to scope to funding persistent teams. In these cases, the plan should identify the key activities required to evolve the approach including updated accountabilities.

- Optimize the approach – PMO teams should look to automate work as well as leverage existing delivery management tools to improve the efficiency of the functions. There are often delivery systems used to coordinate the agile ceremonies and work and they contain the relevant information to aggregate to satisfy stakeholder needs.

The transition plan will likely be part of a larger corporate initiative since it should encompass the entire delivery organization. This plan will also need to include change management activities since the evolution of work will impact resources, accountabilities, organizational functions and stakeholder needs. This could include updated responsibility documents, organizational models and communications. The plan should include the activities listed above along with owners and dates. Once developed the plan should be tracked and managed to completion.

4. Review, learn and iterate

One of the core concepts of scaled agile is continuous learning and improvement. The approach to evolving the PMO functions should also utilize this principle. The team working on the evolving delivery model should establish an approach for reviewing progress and capturing feedback and lessons that can then be incorporated back into the respective delivery teams and PMO functions. The intention should be to continuously look for ways to reduce the amount of governance and administration, automate as many functions as possible, drive delivery transparency and maximize the value of delivery.

Summary

Organizations are looking to optimize their investments in delivery and maximize their velocity towards value realization. These trends are resulting in the need for Portfolio Management Office functions to evolve as well. While some of the functions will be slowed down or even moved into the accountabilities of other delivery areas, the PMO will need to embrace a "lightweight" approach.

Organizations, programs and teams need to develop a deliberate plan to understand the needs, analyze the information and then determine how best to put their PMOs on a diet. The end result should be a significantly leaner PMO that enables transparency of delivery and supports the drive towards value creation and velocity.

6. Aligning Agile and Portfolio Management Principles

The Scaled Agile Framework and portfolio management functions both have guiding principles by which they operate. This chapter will inventory each set of principles and show how they can be aligned to each other.

6.1 Scaled Agile Principles

Chapter 5.2 demonstrated how the PMO functions are evolving within The Scaled Agile Framework is grounded in nine key principles which are core to the model and approach. They are inventoried below (Scaled Agile Framework version 4.5 2018).

1. Take an economic view
2. Apply systems thinking
3. Assume variability; preserve options
4. Build incrementally with fast, integrated learning cycles
5. Base milestones on objective evaluation of working systems
6. Visualize and limit WIP, reduce batch sizes and manage queue lengths

7. Apply cadence, synchronize with cross-domain planning
8. Unlock the intrinsic motivation of knowledge workers
9. Decentralize decision making

This chapter will explore each of these scaled agile principles and then show how they can also be applied to optimize project management, program management and portfolio management concepts and functions.

1. Take an economic view

This principle focuses on aligning all work in the context of the "economies" of value and cost tradeoffs with a focus on early delivery and realization of value. This means that all team members need to have the context for their work and the economic implications of that work.

There are several applications of this principle within the portfolio management functions. The portfolio team should align all scope and work to value so that there is a clear linkage as work gets performed at the different levels of the delivery model. The portfolio also facilitates tradeoffs in prioritization decisions based on value and tradeoffs. The portfolio should also align all of their functions to value realization. Table 6.1 highlights several examples of this alignment.

Table 6.1 Economic view within portfolio functions

Focus	Examples of economic view alignment
Scope Management	• Prioritize and sequence scope that drives the most value the earliest
Financial Management	• Provide transparency into the economics of delivery
Schedule Management	• Align delivery of value as early as possible in an iterative cadence
Reporting	• Align all reporting in the context of value realization
Decisions	• Decisions should be made with the economic impacts clearly identified and understood

Focus	Examples of economic view alignment
Risks and Issues	• Look to remediate and impediments to value as quickly as possible • Understand economic impacts for the realization of risks

Not only should portfolios facilitate this principle within the operations of its functions, but they should embrace it internally as well. When portfolio management functions anchor on the value of the work that they are supporting, they can focus their efforts on providing the relevant transparency and aggregation of information to support that. This then allows them to identify functions or tasks which are not critical and can possibly be reduced in effort, automated or even eliminated.

2. Apply systems thinking

This principle recognizes that work gets performed as a system across many delivery teams and across many areas of an organization and needs to be considered in totality and not just for a particular component or team. Figure 6.1 shows that Scrum Teams can work together on a component which rolls up to an Agile Release Train (which can be considered a system) and then multiple teams and Release Trains can roll up into a Solution Train (which is also a system).

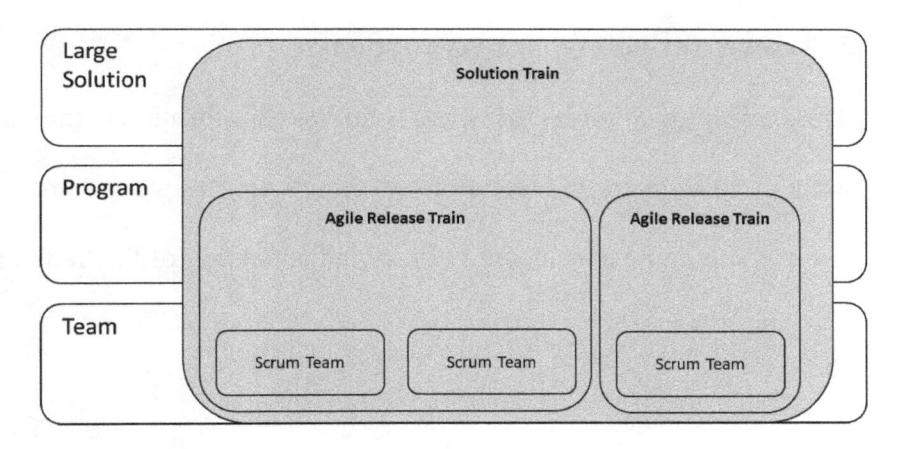

Figure 6.1 Delivery teams aligning around systems

This concept is very important for project management principles because of the product and solution complexity outlined earlier in this book. There are many interdependencies which need to be coordinated across the teams and levels which is where the project management competencies come in. All coordination of work must be performed within the context of the overall solution.

This concept is also significant with respect to how information should be aggregated for end-to-end solutions and higher level scope groupings such as Portfolio Epics. All reporting should align to this concept.

3. Assume variability; preserve options

This concept recognizes that there is not much information known early in the delivery of a solution and therefore multiple design choices should be considered with an understanding of the tradeoffs between them.

For the portfolio function, this means that they need to help facilitate the evaluation of tradeoffs with scope and prioritization across the delivery portfolio and to provide the transparency where there is variability.

This approach can be applied in project management practices when planning for work or solutions. Instead of focusing on one solution, they should be recognizing variability and promoting optionality with solution designs. They can also help to facilitate the tradeoff analysis between the different options.

4. Build incrementally with fast, integrated learning cycles

This principle is fundamental for how work gets planned and delivered in a scaled agile model; in an incremental way through short duration increments to demonstrate capabilities and receive feedback as early as possible.

This principle is applicable to project management concepts because it drives how work should be organized and planned for. As Figure 6.2 shows, planning becomes "bottom up" as a collection of iterations and increments with frequent reviews and retrospectives.

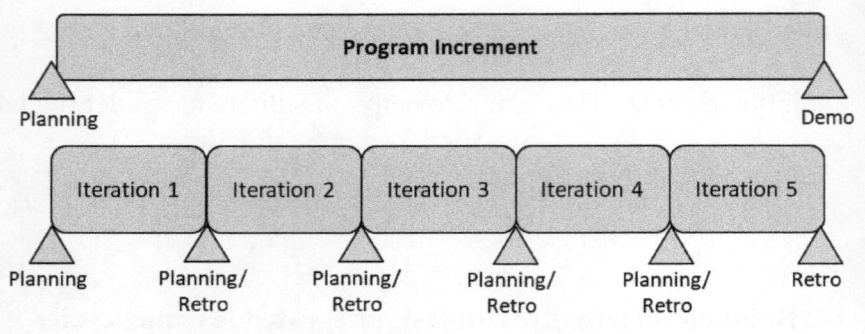

Figure 6.2 Cadence and sequencing of work

Portfolio management functions will need to provide transparency into the progress within the increments and iterations as well as alignment to the broader solution, value and goals.

5. Base milestones on objective evaluation of working systems

Solutions should be reviewed early and often to ensure that the value will be realized, as expected. Demonstrations of working solutions are conducted which show the feasibility of the solution and provide the ability for early feedback to be received and to correct any deviations from expectations. This means that each of the delivery phases happen within each iteration, as compared to the sequential approach of a traditional waterfall model.

Traditionally, PMOs would facilitate phase gate meetings at key delivery milestones. The challenge is that these gates would identify risks later in the delivery lifecycle and, when they were found, they would be costly to remediate since so much work had already been done and time had passed. These frequent iteration reviews require coordination and facilitation across teams and solutions, which requires some of the consultative competencies reviewed in prior chapters.

This approach is applicable to project management concepts as a principle for planning work within the different levels of the delivery model.

- Iterations will require each phase of delivery and the planning should account for this work
- Demonstrations and reviews need to be planned for, coordinated and facilitated
- The feedback from the reviews should be captured and brought back into the teams and backlog

6. Visualize and limit WIP, reduce batch sizes and manage queue lengths

This principle is around the concept of "continuous flow" which includes limiting work in process, reducing the size of work elements and ensuring that queue lengths remain small. These are all concepts that were introduced with the Lean Manufacturing approach of the 1990s.

These lean concepts of continuous flow can be utilized with project management and portfolio management practices as well.

- Look to minimize any work that is piling up; this could be outstanding actions, issues which require attention or decisions that need to be made which are holding up progress
- Ensure that risks and issues get remediated quickly so that progress can continue with a clear understanding of any implications
- Help to break down work into smaller elements which can be delivered quickly
- Look to improve processes which elongate the time for delivery

- Ensure that any outstanding actions get worked on and completed
- Facilitate transparency and reporting of WIP and flow so that improvements can be introduced and measured

7. Apply cadence, synchronize with cross-domain planning

There is a set cadence to delivering in a scaled agile model which includes iterations and increments. This delivery cadence is also aligned to synchronization across multiple stakeholders. These two combine for planning ceremonies at specific intervals with key stakeholders.

PMOs can apply these concepts as well when looking to organize work and facilitate outcomes. Aligning teams to the same cadence and helping to facilitate synchronization will ensure that the delivery teams are all working together towards the appropriate goals and value. A few examples of how PMOs can apply this concept are outlined below:

- Scope should be broken down and aligned into specific delivery iterations (this is done as part of the scope decomposition

process)
- Schedules become a function of coordinating work across iterations and increments
- Reporting, meetings and communications should be aligned to the cadence

8. Unlock the intrinsic motivation of knowledge workers

This principle focuses on empowering team members to be self-directed and understanding what their motivators are. There is recognition that the knowledge workers are experts in their areas of focus and that traditional management top-down motivation is not as effective as intrinsic motivation.

This principle can be applied to the project management evolution as well where project management and PMO functions become focused on supporting the delivery of the team and enabling their success. The aggregation and transparency of information is performed to provide insight into risks and impediments so they can be removed as fast as possible to enable the team to keep moving.

Also, resources that are operating in the key roles identified in Chapter 4.1 (e.g. Scrum Master, Release Train Engineer, etc.) should recognize this need for autonomy and motivation of team members. This should influence how they engage and inspire team members to perform work. This is a change from the traditional top-down approach of project management where resources are told what to do; rather they are now the primary focus as experts in their fields who need to be supported.

9. Decentralize decision making

Lastly, this principle is focused on reducing the delays caused by long decision making processes and targets keeping decisions with the people who are best informed to make them. There are still some centralized decisions which could include decisions around strategy or products.

This concept can be leveraged by project management-type resources that can encourage their team members to make decisions, as appropriate and help to facilitate any cross-team decisions in a rapid manner. They should also help to facilitate the resolution of decisions with the respective accountable role to ensure minimal delay. The PMO can also play a key role in facilitating any centralized or strategic decisions to support the rapid movement towards results and value.

This section has highlighted the nine principles of the Scaled Agile Framework and shown how each one can be applied to portfolio management, program management and project management concepts and functions. Practitioners in these fields should strive to embrace these principles and continuously improve upon them to optimize the efficiency of their teams and speed of delivery.

6.2 Portfolio Management Principles

My second book proposed eight core guiding principles that are required to take a consultative approach to program and portfolio management in today's delivery environment (Wills 2013). This section will provide a brief description of each principle and show how they apply to the Scaled Agile model.

1. Diligence

The first principle focuses on staying on top of all of the moving parts of the program including keeping plans, risk logs, issue logs, action item logs, financials and decisions current, and ensuring that commitments get met. Diligence also means proactively planning ahead which can include understanding vendor contract expirations, resource start dates, and future expenditures to make sure that they are all tracking to the expected plan. Generally, the program manager has to think and track all of these items, so if they are not staying on top of all of them, then most likely they will not get the attention needed and possibly will not be completed on time or accurately.

With regards to scaled agile, diligence is required in many aspects of the operating model:
- Ensuring that progress of work is maintained in the delivery management tool

- Proper identification and tracking of risks, issues and decisions and follow through for their resolution
- Adequate planning for agile ceremonies which could include ensuring work is ready to be demonstrated, logistics planning and coordination of next steps
- Proper facilitation and tracking of scope as it gets prioritized, decomposed and flows down the delivery levels
- Ensuring that intake is managed properly and that backlogs are maintained

2. Attention to Detail

Related to the principle of diligence is the principle of "focusing on the details." While diligence provides structure and a focus on the many moving parts, attention to detail is about understanding the specifics of the activities and making sure that the quality of their output is accurate. Examples of paying attention to details include ensuring that plans are accurate and maintained, risks and issues are updated with appropriate paths to closure, and that scope information reflects the current expectations of stakeholders.

There are many activities within the scaled agile model which require a focus on the details being accurate:

- Maintaining accurate information in the work management system including scope aligned to the proper iteration, progress being updated regularly, acceptance criteria documented and a listing of dependencies
- Ensuring that the scope decomposition has accounted for all expected work and that the scope can be traced through the many delivery layers
- Capturing all relevant information with blockers so that resolution can be done properly and in an informed manner
- Information is accurate which informs decisions or prioritization discussions

3. Transparency

This is a critical principle which focuses on obtaining relevant delivery information and presenting it in a way that allows stakeholders to understand insights, trends and risks to delivery as early indicators of progress. These early insights allow the team to have as much time as possible to take the appropriate action when a risk or issue arises. Examples of transparency include tracking and reporting of milestones, financial variances, risk and issue reporting or the implications of key decisions.

Because of the continuous flow of delivery, transparency is essential to the scaled agile model as well. Several examples of where transparency is needed can be noted.

- Alignment of scope elements to specific teams and delivery iterations
- Progress of work within an iteration or increment (e.g. Kanban board)
- View of what scope is in each backlog and its priority and sequencing
- Velocity of the team (productivity)
- Story points planned and completed for a team within each iteration

4. Single Sources of Truth

Portfolios and programs manage a tremendous amount of information across several different domains. The management of this important information is essential and, in many scenarios, this information gets stored in multiple places and may not always be maintained. The guiding principle of having "single sources of truth" means storing all relevant program information in a single location and keeping it updated and current. Examples include having a single document or location to house information on delivery structure, scope taxonomy, delivery milestones, risks, issues, actions, decisions, resources or finances.

Scaled agile has a few sources of truth that it used to maintain critical delivery information.
- Work intake pipeline to track work intake requests
- Backlogs to maintain team scope information (there are backlogs for each level and scope element)
- Delivery management system to track delivery information,

progress and iterations
- Iteration calendar so all of the teams are working to the same cadence

5. Fact Based Decisions

Facts and relevant information should be used to support timely and accurate decisions. Programs have many decision points which could be related to scope prioritization, option and tradeoff discussions, issue resolution, risk mitigation and solution recommendations. This guiding principle focuses on making decisions effectively and in an informed manner because there is a fact base which supports a specific option or recommendation.

In the scaled agile model, there are also many decision points which require facts to ensure that they get made optimally.
- Portfolio-level decisions on strategic priorities
- Decisions around priorities and sequencing of scope at each level of the model
- Decisions regarding actions to take to remove impediments,

which may have implications on other work

- Team-level decisions for day-to-day activities and solutions

6. The "Ships" in the Fleet of Accountability

I had the clever observation that accountability within the framework of program delivery has three characteristics which all have titles that end in the letters "s", "h", "i" and "p", so I refer to them as the "ships in the fleet of accountability" with the program manager as the captain of this fleet. These characteristics are <u>ownership</u> which means to truly take accountability for the outcomes of the program, <u>stewardship</u> which means to care about the company and program, and <u>leadership</u> which means being a champion and motivator for the program team.

These characteristics of accountability are also evident in the scaled agile model within several roles and functions.

- A focus on value exemplifies the concept of stewardship back to the company
- Product Owners should have accountability for scope and

prioritization decisions

- Many scaled agile roles require leadership qualities including Scrum Master, Release Train Engineer and Solution Train Engineer

7. Simplicity

The principle of "simplicity" is about ensuring that processes, products, technology solutions and organizations are kept as simple as possible to avoid complexity, risk, quality issues, cost and confusion. Related to delivery, complexity in any of these areas easily results in additional cost, higher probability of issues and risks and a higher probability of quality problems. A relevant quote comes from Antoine de Saint-Exupery when he says that "It seems that perfection is achieved not when there is nothing more to add, but when there is nothing more to take away." He said this nearly one century ago and it is still very relevant today.

In scaled agile, this principle is embedded in the concept of "minimum viable product" which is taking the least amount of work required to deliver on a solution. Simplicity is also a key tenant of lean portfolio management which focuses on focusing the portfolio functions on high value activities with the use of automation and delivery management systems.

8. Taking a customer focused approach

The final guiding principle focuses on the acknowledgement that many interactions within delivery have a customer relationship and should be treated as such. For example, developers are a customer of the design team when delivering solution documents. Viewing people or teams as one's customer makes people perceive the interaction differently and bring more of a sense of service quality to the relationship.

There are also several customer relationships within the scaled agile model.
- Many delivery teams are customers of each other with respect to interdependent components of a solution
- The teams on the lower levels of the model are customers of

scope decomposition as it flows down

- The teams on the upper levels of the model are customers of information as it flows up
- Delivery teams are customers of shared services organizations and functions

6.3 Aligning the Principles

The scaled agile principles and program management principles do overlap with each other and are very much interconnected. Figure 6.3 and Figure 6.4 demonstrate a mapping between the agile principles (rows) and the program management ones (columns).

	Diligence	Attention to Detail	Transparency	Single Source
Economic View	Tracking of economics and tradeoffs	Ensure economic details are accurate	Clarity of economics, value and tradeoffs	Track all economic information in one place
Systems Thinking	Coordinate all interdepent aspects of the system	Accurate details regarding system components	Clarity of what the system is comprised of and how it is progressing	Key system information tracked in a single location
Variablity, Options	Planning for several options	Ensuring option details are correct	Clarity where there is variability and of optionality	Track options, impacts and decisions in one place
Incremental Build	Tracking increment information	Keeping iteration specifics maintained	Clarity of progress in increments and plans	Standard increment calendar and alignment of scope
Objective Eval	Planning and conducting demos	Accurate information within demo	Clarity of information in demos	Central tracking of demo information and actions
Limit WIP, Batch, Queue	Removal of barriers to ensure continuos flow	Knowing details which drive and impact flow	Metrics around flow, size and WIP	Tracking of flow information in one location
Cadence, Synch	Provide structure in cadence and ceremonies	Ensure iteration information is accurate	Publish calendars and information from ceremonies	Single view of cadence and stakeholders
Motivation of Workers	Stay diligent with motivating team	Understand details of what motivates team	Provide team insights so they understand	Provide single sources of information to team
Decentralized Decisions	Tracking decision information	Accurate insights to inform decisions	Outcomes of decisions	Decision repository

Figure 6.3 – Alignment of Principles (Part 1)

	Fact Based	Ships	Simplicity	Customer Focus
Economic View	Use facts to support tradeoff decisions	Take ownership of economics; value drives stewardship	Focus on main value and tradeoffs	Recognize who is the customer of value and who is impacted
Systems Thinking	System information is accurate and updated	Taking ownership for the complete system end-to-end	Focusing on minimal viable product of the system	Clarity of who the customers of the system are as well as the components
Variablity, Options	Use facts to determine best option	Taking ownership of options and stewardship for impacts	Focusing on minium set of options for variability	Recognizing customer impacts of tradeoffs
Incremental Build	Velocity and storypoints to drive planning	Taking accountability for planned work in increments	Minimal solutions should be planned in	Idnetify customers who drive acceptance criteria
Objective Eval	Demonstrate working functionality	Stewardship through sharing demos	Keep demos focused on key points	Identify audience and their interests of demos
Limit WIP, Batch, Queue	Using actual metics to track flow	Accountabiliy for flow and improvements	Simplify to optimize WIP, batch and queues	Each handoff has a customer
Cadence, Synch	Facts to inform ceremonies	Ownership of work in cadence	Keep calendar and approach simple and focused	Recognize customers of each ceremony and activity
Motivation of Workers	Rely on expertise to extract facts	Leading and motivating teams	Simplify workers jobs	Treat team members as customers
Decentralized Decisions	Facts to support informed decisions	Ownership of decisions	Focusing on relevant information	Understanding stakeholders of impacts

Figure 6.4 – Alignment of Principles (Part 2)

These charts are very enlightening and clearly demonstrate that the two sets of principles are complimentary to each other and support each other. This means that the belief that program management is at odds with scaled agile is incorrect and should be modified to recognize that they are very much aligned. Not only are they aligned but they should be planned together to optimize the value and effectiveness of the delivery teams.

7. Key Concepts

This book has covered many topics within the evolving landscape of technology delivery and the alignment of scaled agile and project management principles and concepts. Throughout the book there are several key concepts and themes which have arisen. This chapter highlights these concepts as a way to summarize the points and draw some relevant conclusions.

7.1 The Delivery Model has Changed

Scaled agile has fundamentally changed the model for delivery of work. Figure 7.1 demonstrates the differences between the traditional approach and the scaled agile approach. A traditional model operates in a top down model, working from the Portfolio to the Program and then the Projects. Program managers and project managers centralize control and manage plans, financials and risks/issues. Information is coordinated and shared through status meetings with many stakeholders. A PMO is used to collect key information and report against it.

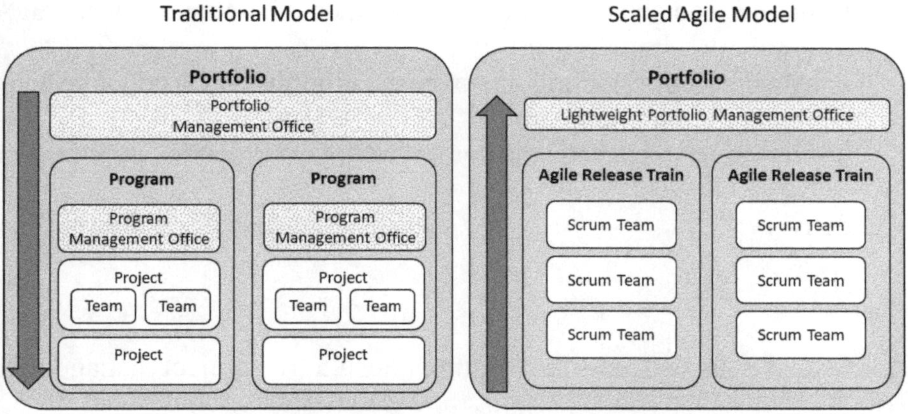

Figure 7.1 Evolved delivery model

In the scaled agile model, the approach is very much bottom-up focused on scrum teams. While scope decomposes down, the work and information aggregates up the model. Project management type resources are used to coordinate work across teams and facilitate the key ceremonies. A lightweight portfolio management office is used to aggregate information for transparency and facilitate strategic planning.

7.2 It is Not an "or" Conversation

Throughout this book, there have been many examples which demonstrate that scaled agile principles and project management principles can coexist and evolve together. Therefore, it is not an "or" conversation of selecting one over the other but an "and" conversation of how we can leverage the combined set of principles for successful delivery.

Scaled agile concepts still require consultative project management competencies. Several examples where these competencies are needed are highlighted below:

- Planning and coordination of iterations and stakeholder demonstrations
- Alignment and tracking of scope elements to strategies and value realization
- Facilitation of agile ceremonies
- Coordination of milestones and dependencies across teams and solutions
- Facilitation of risk and issue identification, escalation and remediation
- Diligence in tracking progress, dependencies and impediments in delivery management tools

- Facilitation of rapid decisions
- Communication to key stakeholders
- Leading and motivating the team to optimize efficiency and value delivery

Scaled agile delivery also requires many PMO functions even though their focus evolves. There are several examples of these evolved functions.

- Scope decomposition and prioritization through the many delivery levels
- Alignment of funding to persistent teams and no longer specific scope
- Reduced need for resource management since resources are dedicated to persistent teams
- Facilitation of escalated risks and issues to resolution in a timely manner
- Coordination of milestones and dependencies across delivery teams and solutions
- Communication to portfolio-level stakeholders

- Facilitation of key strategic decisions and portfolio-level prioritization
- Facilitation of key agile ceremonies aligned to the cadence timeframes

There is significant value realized with the combination of the two sets of practices. Project management principles provide coordination and facilitation across complex inter-related solutions, transparency into progress and diligence to ensure that all open items get addressed. Agile principles focus on maximizing value, a focus on the teams and continuous delivery. Table 7.1 highlights several examples where the two sets of practices combine to optimize the value and success of delivery.

Table 7.1 Value of combined practices

Focus	Project Mgt	Scaled Agile	Value
Scope Alignment	Planning and organization of work	Decomposition of work and prioritization of value	Clear structure of scope and alignment to value
Schedule	Coordination of dependencies and diligence of tracking	Cadence of iterations and ceremonies	Successful coordination of many moving parts with early delivery of value
Decisions	Diligence and facilitation	Empowered teams with decentralized power	Rapid, but informed, decisions

Focus	Project Mgt	Scaled Agile	Value
Risks and Issues	Facilitation of teams and follow through	Ceremonies for teams to identify risks early	Early identification and closure of risks to minimize impact
Team Morale	Motivation, structure and leadership	Empowered teams and servant leadership	High quality of delivery through motivated teams
Value Realization	Facilitation and coordination of work	Demonstrations and ceremonies	Early feedback on value and ability to correct

Focus	Project Mgt	Scaled Agile	Value
Quality	Connecting the dots across teams and solutions	Systems thinking and ceremonies	Better end to end products and solutions
Ceremonies	Facilitation and diligence	Agile ceremonies and practices	Better outcomes from ceremonies
Insights	Transparency and diligence in tracking	Use of delivery management tools as part of working	Better insights into progress and risks

7.3 Agile is Not an Excuse

Many companies are transitioning to a scaled agile model and while I do understand the core agile principles, my observation is that sometimes people can use "agile" as an excuse to not have fundamental tenants of success. The top three that come to mind are highlighted below:

1. A vision is still needed

Agility is about iterating and prioritizing, but it has to be in the context of an overall vision. Without that, the team will constantly be re-prioritizing and spinning and nothing will get accomplished. Getting nowhere quickly because of agile does not sound right, and so a vision is critical.

2. Leadership is still needed

Once the vision is clear, leaders need to drive that vision and champion it throughout the organization. While agile promotes teams and delegated work, leadership is still needed to "connect the dots", provide direction and remove impediments. I do not believe that large corporations can ever move to fully federated models where teams just "do stuff" and naturally come together, collaborate and understand interdependencies (i.e. the premise of teams not performing magic).

3. Project management competencies are still needed

While there are no formal project management roles in agile, there is clearly a need for the competencies which make someone a successful project management. There is still the need for facilitation, negotiation, communication, planning, escalations and other critical competencies. There is also a need for managing interdependencies and complexities of the work.

Without these three things I see companies having significant challenges which can't really be justified under the header of "that is an agile approach to fail and learn." There is failing based on taking risks and trying and then there is failing because of stupidity and we should recognize the difference.

7.4 Anchor on the Principles and Align Coaching

Project management is not an exact science and neither is the scaled agile practice. Because every company and culture is different, we will need anchor on the principles of scaled agile. The same prescription that works for one company may not work for another company.

We have to understand the corporate culture, organizational politics and policies of our companies and then look to apply the scaled agile (and project management) principles. This is why so many agile coaches offer counsel but do not tell team members what to do; there is not meant to be a prescriptive approach for how to implement scaled agile.

However, I do believe that the model of coaching needs to also evolve and align to both sets of principles. It is not enough to simply advise on how to perform agile ceremonies. I believe that the coaching model needs to become more consultative and look for ways to optimize team performance in accordance with program management and scaled agile concepts. Some examples of areas to support include the following:

- Is the team and delivery organization structure optimal for delivery?

- Are the team members diligent in maintaining key delivery information in the appropriate system?
- Are the ceremonies planned for and executed properly and how could they be improved?
- Do the resources in key delivery roles have and demonstrate the appropriate competencies or do they need to be supplemented somehow?
- Are the solutions and systems being managed properly across the teams?

On order for coaches to be able to assess and support these areas they need to possess the relevant experience themselves. I have seen cases where coaches seem to be people who have memorized the Scaled Agile Framework and simply espouse verse. Coaches can be a valuable component to the model but these roles need to become more consultative to recognize inefficiencies and help support their optimization.

7.5 It Has Always Been About the People

Whether we are discussing project management or scaled agile, the fundamental truth is that success is based on the people and team members who are performing the work. In the introduction to The Team Handbook, W. Edwards Deming wrote that "The system that people work in and the interaction with people may account for 90 or 95 percent of performance." (Scholtes 2003).

Focusing on obtaining and growing the right talent with the right competencies will make teams and organizations significantly more successful than introducing new processes or tools. Therefore, organizations should invest in talent identification, training and retention. In my prior book on competencies, I introduced a framework for companies to improve organizational competencies which is shown on Figure 7.2 (Wills 2017).

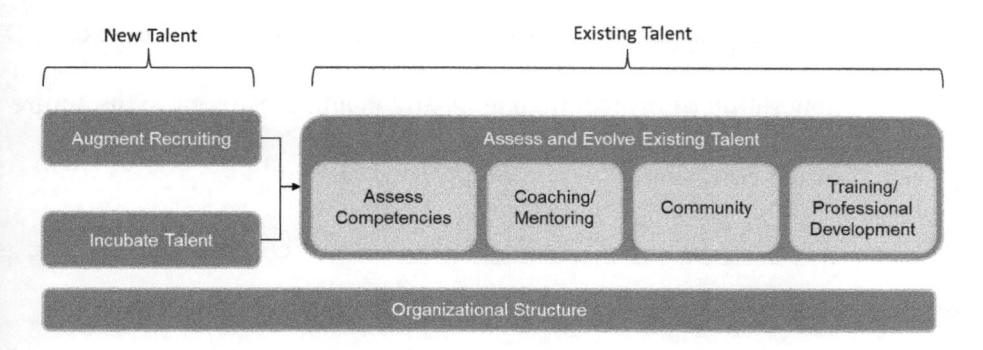

Figure 7.2 Competency improvement approach

The talent improvement approach should include several main elements in order to be comprehensive. The first two elements focus on bringing and growing new talent, the next element focuses on the existing pool of resources and the last area of focus is the organizational structure.

- <u>Augment Recruiting</u> – A focus on recruiting affects the types of project managers that get hired into an organization. In some cases, it may be more effective to hire people with the right skills than it would be to augment the skills of current resources.
- <u>Incubate Talent</u> – The approach should also have a deliberate strategy for bringing in newer resources and growing them. This could be in a leadership program or just a focused effort for

college graduates. Incubating talent means growing the next generation of project managers and is an investment in the future of the company.

- <u>Assess and Evolve Existing Talent</u> – Most companies have a large pool of delivery resources and the approach should consider the best ways to improve the competencies of the existing resources. This may start with a competency assessment to get a sense of where there may be individual or organizational gaps. Then an action plan could include mentoring, coaching, training or even movement of resources. Note that sometimes team members are not the right fit for a particular role and the organization may need to consider how to optimally align resources to the work to build on their strengths which could include moving people to different roles.
- <u>Organizational Structure</u> – The structure of an organization has an impact on what competencies are most needed and should be optimized to allow for effective delivery of work. This can include grouping shared services into organizations and aligning delivery teams together.

If companies want to optimize their return on an investment in scaled agile, then they should have a comprehensive talent strategy as part of that initiative.

7.6 Revisit the Hypotheses and Conclusions

Chapter 2.4 introduced four hypotheses regarding project management concepts within scaled agile which the content of this book sought to prove. Over the course of the book, key points were made and examples were given to demonstrate these hypotheses. This section will summarize those findings.

1. There are still projects, but their definition changes

Chapter 3 showed how scope decomposes down the scaled agile model and then key information is aggregated up to provide transparency at each level. Portfolio Epics were identified as a critical element which had many of the same characteristics as a project; aligned to strategy, has an identified owner, spans multiple teams and has a business case.

While a Portfolio Epic may have similar attributes to a traditional project, the operating model is different. Rather than a top-down grouping of a funded amount of finite scope, the Portfolio Epics are aggregations of prioritized scope and funding of the dedicated teams working on that scope. They are also more fluid with the specific detailed scope being prioritized and sequenced.

2. There is still the need for project management competencies

Chapter 4 acknowledged that there are no formal roles that contain the title of project manager in scaled agile models. However, the case was made that the complexity of delivery is increasing and with the agile principle of small teams the net result would be a large number of interdependent teams. Since these self-organizing teams do not necessarily "perform magic" and may require unnatural acts for some team members there is a need for roles to coordinate across teams and interdependencies.

Five key scaled agile roles were identified with a description of each of their responsibilities. These responsibilities were then compared to a framework of consultative project management competencies and mapped together in a matrix. The clear conclusion is that this same set of competencies is critical for success of the scaled agile roles. It was noted that there is not a clear translation of a project management role to a scaled agile role and that it should be the competencies of the individual resource which would determine the most appropriate role for them.

3. **There is still the need for portfolio management office functions, but they evolve**

Chapter 5 identified that there is still the need for PMO functions, but that they need to evolve. The corporate environment is one that requires transparency of strategic roadmaps, the need to prioritize across many initiatives and a need for metrics such as return on investment so there will still be the need for functions to track this information. However, the operating model with scaled agile changes how each of these functions performs.

Portfolio management functions also need to focus on becoming more lightweight where there is a focus on value and supporting delivery needs. An approach was outlines to put our PMOs on a diet to make them leaner which included automation, the use of tools and eliminating non-value added processes.

4. The agile principles can be applied to project and portfolio management

Lastly, the nine key principles of scaled agile were outlined in Chapter 6. Each of these was described and then examples were given on how to apply them to portfolio management and project management functions. This demonstrated that agile principles and project management principles could be combined to realize significant value.

Conclusion

Hopefully this book accomplished its goals which were to encourage a dialogue between the project management world and the scaled agile world, prove four key hypotheses regarding project management in a scaled agile model and to demonstrate that it does not have to be either model; they can both exist and are actually more impactful when combined together.

References

Kent Beck; James Grenning; Robert C. Martin; Mike Beedle; Jim Highsmith; Steve Mellor; Arie van Bennekum; Andrew Hunt; Ken Schwaber; Alistair Cockburn; Ron Jeffries; Jeff Sutherland; Ward Cunningham; Jon Kern; Dave Thomas; Martin Fowler; Brian Marick (2001). "Manifesto for Agile Software Development". Agile Alliance. Retrieved 14 June 2010

Scholtes, Peter R (2003). *The Team Handbook Third Edition.* Madison, Wisconsin: Oriel Incorporated

Leffingwell, Dean. "Scaled Agile Framework – SAFe for Lean Software and System Engineering." Scaled Agile Framework, 3 Jan. 2016. Web. 01 Feb. 2017

Scaled Agile Framework. (2018). Retrieved from www.scaledagileframework.com

Wills, Kerry R. (2013). *Applying Guiding Principles of Effective Program Delivery*. Taylor & Francis. Boca Raton, Florida

Wills, Kerry R. (2017). *The Consultative PM: An Evolved Model for Project Management Competencies*. Lulu.com

CPSIA information can be obtained
at www.ICGtesting.com
Printed in the USA
LVHW111301140720
660678LV00009B/62